LOST IN THE MUSEUM

BURIED TREASURES AND THE STORIES THEY TELL

Nancy Moses

ALTAMIRA
PRESS

ALTAMIRA PRESS
A division of Rowman & Littlefield Publishers, Inc.
A wholly owned subsidary of
The Rowman & Littlefield Publishing Group, Inc.
4501 Forbes Boulevard, Suite 200, Lanham, MD 20706
www.altamirapress.com

Estover Road, Plymouth PL6 7PY, United Kingdom

British Library Cataloguing in Publication Information Available

Library of Congress Cataloging-in-Publication Data

Moses, Nancy, 1948–
  Lost in the museum : buried treasures and the stories they tell /
Nancy Moses.
      p. cm.
  Includes bibliographical references and index.
  ISBN-13: 978-0-7591-1069-4 (cloth : alk. paper)
  ISBN-10: 0-7591-1069-7 (cloth : alk. paper)
  ISBN-13: 978-0-7591-1070-0 (pbk. : alk. paper)
  ISBN-10: 0-7591-1070-0 (pbk. : alk. paper)
  1. Museums—Collection management. 2. Museums—Collection
management—United States. 3. Museums—United States. 4. Museums—
Pennsylvania—Philadelphia Region. I. Title.

  AM133.M67 2008
  069'.5—dc22

                                                        2007028366

Printed in the United States of America

∞™ The paper used in this publication meets the minimum requirements of
American National Standard for Information Sciences—Permanence of Paper
for Printed Library Materials, ANSI/NISO Z39.48-1992.

5/09 ③ 7/09
5 x 7/11 (8/19)

LOST IN THE
MUSEUM

To Myron, my rock

CONTENTS

ACKNOWLEDGMENTS ix

INTRODUCTION "The Stuff" 1

1 **JOHN JAMES AUDUBON'S BIRDS** 9
   Academy of Natural Sciences

2 **BLASCHKA SEA ANIMALS** 23
   Carnegie Museums of Pittsburgh

3 **FRANKLIN B. GOWEN'S BOWL** 39
   Historical Society of Pennsylvania

4 **PESSARIES** 57
   Mütter Museum of the College of Physicians
     of Philadelphia

5 **SKULL OF A PREHISTORIC
   PERUVIAN CHILD** 69
   Smithsonian Institution, National Museum
     of Natural History

6 **KER-FEAL** 85
   Barnes Foundation

7 **PLAN FOR THE DOME OF THE
   UNITED STATES CAPITOL** 101
   Athenaeum of Philadelphia

8   **JOHN BROWN'S PIKE**   117
     Civil War and Underground Railroad Museum
         of Philadelphia

9   **SUMMER GARMENTS OF A
     TIBETAN PRINCESS**   133
     Burke Museum of Natural History and Culture

EPILOGUE   151

**RESOURCES: FOR THOSE WHO WANT
     TO LEARN MORE**   155

INDEX   159

ABOUT THE AUTHOR   167

ACKNOWLEDGMENTS

Many people generously gave their time and talent during the years I spent writing *Lost in the Museum*. A number are already cited in the text, and I wish to thank each one. In addition are those who helped on individual chapters: Dr. Robert Peck and Dr. D. James Baker (Academy of Natural Sciences); Dr. Morris Kricun and Virginia Kricun, who introduced me to Donald Ortner (Smithsonian Institution, National Museum of Natural History); Dr. George Wohlreich (Mütter Museum of the College of Physicians of Philadelphia); Robert Gangewere (Carnegie Museums of Pittsburgh); Katy Rawdon-Faucett and Derek Gillman (Barnes Foundation); Hyman Myers, AIA, and Bruce Laverty (Athenaeum of Philadelphia); and Dr. John Rumm (Civil War and Underground Railroad Museum of Philadelphia). Ingrid Bogel and Glen Ruzicka of the Conservation Center for Art and Historic Artifacts helped to clarify some of the finer points of conservation, and Randi Kamine checked the facts.

I could not have done without the encouragement of Keith Talbot and Mary Hagy, the editorial support of Julie Liedman and Mary Gregg, and the insightful comments of Bob Barnett and Rochelle Magarick. Many thanks also to Meredith Brossard and Dr. Thomas Reiner, who read the manuscript early and at the end of the process. I appreciate the patience and confidence in me evidenced by Jack Meinhardt and Serena Krombach, my editors at AltaMira Press. Finally, there will always be a special place in my heart for Jean Rowlands Tarbox, who never doubted I would finish this book, though I often doubted it myself.

INTRODUCTION
"The Stuff"

Floor to ceiling, wall to wall, lining the long metal shelves were At-water Kent radios, obsolete kitchen appliances, patent models of never-built inventions, guns, and butter churns. A life-size mannequin in a faded gray gown sat on a top shelf, her head tipped back, her arms akimbo. Advertising signs and wooden hangers from long-bankrupt department stores covered a wall. Thomas Alva Edison's records—cylinders made of wax—stood near the phonograph that once made them sing. Each object had tiny numbers inscribed on it or on a small attached tag.

When he talked to outsiders, Jeffrey Ray, curator of collections, called these objects "the precious treasures of Philadelphia's past." Alone with us insiders, he called them "the stuff."

It's this stuff that fills not only the attic and basement of the Atwater Kent Museum but of almost every collecting institution—every museum, historic house, archive, and special collection library—in the world. Children's museums store toys and baby furniture; science museums store inventions; art museums store the work of artists, major and minor. Though not alive, the stuff is voracious; unless carefully checked, it will devour the budget. Collecting institutions can spend more time, energy, and money caring for the mountains of stuff that nobody sees than they spend on public exhibits.

I must confess, I love stuff. When I was no older than five or six, my mother would take me on excursions. One day we'd go to the Carnegie Institute—the sprawling brick building that housed Pittsburgh's art and natural history museums—the next day to an antique shop. Museums and antique shops seemed pretty similar to me. Both were filled with stuff, though you could take things home from the antique shop.

People are fascinated with stuff, which is why there are so many museums and museum visitors: about 865 million a year, more than attend all professional sport games combined. That's also why there are so many types of stuff. There are artifacts made by human hands, relics with spiritual meanings, charms with magical powers, talismans to bring good luck, souvenirs, artworks, mementos, specimens of flora and fauna, and many, many types of documents. Heirlooms are passed from generation to generation and sometimes end up in an archive.

These objects are very powerful, infused with meaning, for they tell us who we are as individuals and as a society; they connect us with our past. When we save objects, we allow future generations to view them through the fresh lens of their times and life experiences.

Although I had a graduate degree in American Studies with a specialty in Material Culture, and had served museums as clients in my marketing communications firm, I'd never worked in one until I accepted the position of executive director of the Atwater Kent Museum. Flush with anticipation during my first week on the job, I called a meeting of the curatorial staff. I smiled hopefully at the six people sitting around the table.

"How does an object become a museum artifact?" I asked. The staff stared back at me, their eyes clearly communicating, "Wherever did the board of directors find this one?"

Jeffrey Ray, a dapper fellow with a strawberry blond mustache, peered over the glasses perched at the tip of his nose and took a deep breath. "You can tell a museum artifact because it has an accession number written on it," he said. "When a museum accepts an object, it assigns an accession number." He reached for the metal toy train engine in the middle of the table, pointing out the tiny number painted on its side.

I pondered this for a moment.

"What about yesterday's toast?" I asked. "If yesterday's toast had a number on it, would the museum have to care for it?"

"Yep," piped the assistant curator. "If the toast has a number on it, it's part of the collection, and we're responsible for it forever."

While the Atwater Kent Museum had never accessioned a piece of toast, it did own much that seemed almost as irrelevant. Stained petticoats from the colonial era. Victorian chairs oozing stuffing. Dingy paintings in broken picture frames. The sorry remains of a department store Christmas display that had once captivated generations of children. Jeffrey Ray proudly called the collection "eclectic." Some of what I saw fit a less flattering description. I was haunted by evil fantasies in which I pulled up a truck to the museum in the dead of night, piled in the worst of the stuff, and dumped it in the Schuylkill River.

I'd taken the job at the toughest time in the fifty-year history of this museum of city history. The city of Philadelphia financed the lion's share of its budget, but the city was going broke. Faced with a possible municipal bankruptcy, the mayor had decided to erase the Atwater Kent from the budget. The place was virtually empty; nobody came. And if nobody came, the mayor reasoned, why keep it open?

I was hired to save the place, to change the mayor's mind. Unless we brought more people through the doors, the doors would close forever. Though I lacked museum management experience, my marketing expertise appealed in these desperate times. I seemed—to myself and to the board of directors that hired me—the perfect person to rescue and revitalize the Atwater Kent.

But the galleries were tired and tiny: most museums display about 10 percent of their holdings, but our galleries were so small that we could exhibit only 1 percent of what we owned. The 80,000 items in the collection were desperate for tender, loving care. Though some seemed of questionable merit, there was much that was deserving of it. Among the treasures were thousands of images documenting Philadelphia's changing landscape, elegant bridal and ball gowns worn by generations of local ladies, relics harvested by soldiers on Civil War battlefields, and the thank-you gift that traitor Aaron Burr gave to his Philadelphia in-laws who hid him and his wife during the American Revolution.

Millions were needed to care for the stuff: new equipment to keep the temperature and humidity constant, new computer hardware and software to keep track of it all. At museums, everything seems to cost more. A roof suitable for a national landmark building costs four times as much as an ordinary roof, a museum-quality storage box that won't destroy the flag or book inside costs ten times the same box at an office supply store.

The challenge was huge, the resources few. Moreover, from a business perspective, the business model didn't add up. Soon after I began at the Atwater Kent Museum, I was shocked to learn that earned income from ticket sales, store sales, the summer camp, and school groups covered only 15 percent of the operating budget. That meant we had to find eighty-five cents on every dollar from somewhere else. Many museums have endowments that fill the gap. We didn't. The Atwater Kent was essentially a cash business with an out-of-date product, a limited customer base, and no cash reserve.

Many directors burn out. I quickly learned why.

These seemingly serene places are extraordinarily complicated. Museum directors, to be truly effective, must combine the aesthetic instincts of an artist, the intellectual muscle of a scholar, the negotiating skills of a diplomat, the flash of an impresario, and the business savvy of a corporate CEO. They must entice visitors with stunning artwork, spectacular exhibits, provocative programs, elegant restaurants, and attractive store merchandise. They must satisfy the needs of their multiple constituents, the often unrealistic expectations of their staff, the egos of their donors, and the desires of their boards of trustees.

The toughest challenge museums face is balancing the often competing missions: educating the public with exhibits and programs, serving researchers and scholars, and properly preserving the holdings. Whether their revenue comes from government, foundations, donors, endowments, or ticket sales—or as is usually the case, a mix of all of these—there's never enough. With limited resources, it's tough to choose among competing priorities, and tougher still to keep to the plan. Every day brings seductive new opportunities and unpleasant surprises: a broken elevator, a leaky basement.

Finally, museums must constantly struggle to remain relevant to the ever-changing contours of the community outside their doors. Unless collecting institutions do more than collect, unless they actively contribute to the lives of their communities, they become irrelevant and thus unworthy of public support.

As the new executive director of one of these exasperatingly complex institutions, I pondered these challenges in light of our urgent need for survival. Over time, the strategy came clear. Strengthen the appeal of the product: the exhibits and programs. Build the customer base. And do everything possible to increase revenues. I shared the strategy with the board and staff, and we got to work.

The first assignment was to produce winning exhibits and programs. With a donation from a generous board member, we conducted market research with key audiences: parents of school-age children, teachers, and tourist officials. That research yielded a list of exhibit topics for the new market-driven agenda. We staged an exhibit created by school-children. We displayed the work of the wildly popular Norman Rockwell to draw tourists. We put together a show of political memorabilia that opened during the Republican National Convention. We produced summer concerts, an annual tribute to local businesses celebrating major anniversaries, and a tea party to tie into Philadelphia's annual restaurant festival.

The second challenge was to build the customer base, or in museum parlance, the "stakeholders." Atwater Kent's stakeholders included not only the visitors and school groups, but also the politicians who controlled the budget, the hospitality industry who served the tourists, and the media. City council members, hotel concierges, and taxi drivers were invited in to get to know us. Fifteen percent of the tiny budget was invested in advertising, direct mail, and media promotions, and on a new marketing director with myriad media contacts.

At the same time, we focused on money: finding it, raising it, and making it. Finding it was the most fun. The Atwater Kent is a city government agency, which means piles of forms and miles of red tape. At first, the city connection appeared a liability, but as it turned out, it was a huge, untapped asset. A municipal employee was assigned to prowl the bowels of the bureaucracy and locate essential resources. Soon, the museum benefited from free postage, a new telephone system, and a much-needed renovation of our dated galleries. When everything we got free as a city government agency was added up, the budget was actually more than $1 million. That placed us in the top ranks of history museums in all of Pennsylvania. We were players.

Raising money was tougher because the competition for grants and donations was so stiff and our profile was so low. My days were devoted to writing grant proposals and squeezing the last dollar out of the budget; my evenings were spent at cocktail receptions trying to charm donations from the rich and powerful.

Making money was the most challenging, but also the most essential, since the money that a museum earns can be used for anything it needs. We became cultural entrepreneurs. With a foundation grant, we purchased a tent for the garden, which we rented out for social events and uscd for the concert series. An expert assessed the small museum shop, upgraded the merchandise, and extended the hours.

The board stepped forward to help: the chairman spent hours coaching me in not-for-profit management; the treasurer helped balance the books; the scholars advised on exhibits, collection guidelines, and educational programs. They also helped to recruit new board members with deeper pockets and more direct access to the mayor.

Unfortunately, while all this was happening, the collections slid down the list of priorities. They hung as heavy as an albatross around my neck. The curators needed to complete the collections inventory; we needed them to work on exhibits. I loved accompanying curator Jeffrey Ray as he escorted a visitor inside the storage crypt, reached for an artifact, and spun a tale that brought it back to life. I dreaded spending money to care for it.

Through sleepless nights I asked myself, did other museum directors struggle with the same problems I faced? How were they able to satisfy today's public and still preserve their treasures for posterity? Why *do* collecting institutions collect so much more than they're ever able to display?

Three exhausting years later, I resigned as director of the Atwater Kent Museum. Through ingenuity and a lot of hard work, the staff had managed to create captivating new offerings that more than doubled attendance. Television features and newspaper stories celebrated the exciting new things happening at this once tired old museum. The best news of all was that the mayor changed his mind. The museum's doors would remain open.

I'd opted to invest in exhibits over collections. The public was pleased; the curators were not. We met the challenge of survival, but at the cost of improving the care of our unwieldy, eclectic holdings.

As it turned out, the Atwater Kent's struggles to care for its holdings were symptomatic of a national crisis. A 2006 report by Heritage Preservation and the Institute of Museum and Library Services found that America's 30,000 collecting institutions hold 4.8 billion items. Huge mountains of the stuff—270 million books, journals, and newspapers; 189 million scientific specimens; 153 million photographs; 13.5 million historic objects; 4.7 million works of art—need immediate attention. No one knows how many billions of dollars it would cost to properly preserve it all, let alone where the money would come from.

But, unless there's some fast action, much of our precious material heritage may be lost forever.

Freed from the daily rigors of a manager's job, I decided to search for answers to the questions that had corroded my sleep. Over the next few years I called the directors of some of my favorite collecting institutions and asked to see an item with an interesting back-story but that had seldom, if ever, been placed on display. In every case, the director knew just what I wanted and was eager to show it to me. At each place I discovered not only an object with a captivating human story but also a jigsaw piece in the puzzle of problems I found while managing a museum.

While storage vaults all over the world are crammed with stuff, Philadelphia was an excellent place to begin my search for hidden treasures. The region has more history museums, historical sites, and historical societies than any place in the nation. There are museums about urban, religious, medical, and natural history; art and decorative art; African American culture; archeology; science and technology; firefighters; shoes; and Betsy Ross. There's even a museum dedicated to the uniquely Philadelphian, feather-wearing, cross-dressing Mummers, who strut up the city's main boulevard, sometimes intoxicated, every New Year's Day. There are nationally important museums of art, natural history, and archeology. There are historic houses once occupied by the nation's founders, deranged generals, and famous musicians; outstanding archives and libraries; and America's most cherished shrines to democracy: Independence Hall and the Liberty Bell.

Philadelphia is where the modern museum was born. It was home to the nation's first public museum, founded by Charles Willson Peale soon after the American Revolution. Dedicated to revealing the wonders of America to the American public, Peale filled his museum with what today seems an odd assortment of items: stuffed birds, animal bones, and portraits by the great artist himself. Housed on the second floor of the State House, now called Independence Hall, Peale's museum was an instant success. Like the new nation itself, it was something new on earth: a place open to all, not just the elite.

While Peale's museum is long gone, its legacy survives; in fact, it's become a major industry. In Greater Philadelphia, tourism drives the economy, generating almost $7 billion in 2004, and museums and historic sites are why most tourists come.

I've worked in Philadelphia for thirty years, much of it in and around the cultural tourism industry. My access to museum directors opened backroom doors usually shut to outsiders. So it made sense to explore Philadelphia and then travel to museums in cities beyond to see what was buried in their crypts.

I soon realized that museums objects were more than paintings, paper, wood, and pottery. Each was infused with greater meaning that spoke to its time and ours. A gorgeous rendering of the dome of the United States Capitol building revealed the aesthetic and engineering genius—and political tribulations—of Thomas Ustick Walter, the most influential architect of mid-nineteenth-century America. Four bird carcasses caught, stuffed, and painted by John James Audubon and now held in a storeroom drawer connected to art, science, and the era of discovery when this nation was young.

Some objects told darker stories: stories of political intrigue, legal battles, and ethical dilemmas. A wicked-looking pike in the basement of a townhouse museum brought back to life John Brown's quixotic quest to free the slaves. A golden and silver trophy bowl held the sinister tale of Franklin Benjamin Gowen, the treacherous robber baron who destroyed one of America's first labor unions. A Tibetan princess's elegant garments held the story of her and her family's perilous flight from the invading Chinese communists, intent on destroying their ancient society.

This book follows my journey beyond the crowded galleries, high-tech, interactive contraptions, and chic museum shops, through the "employees only" doors, and into the silence of the crypts. While these vaults were stuffed with stuff that was irrelevant, duplicative, and marginally significant, there was also much that was fascinating and rare. There's nothing to compare with the thrill of holding in your hands the thousand-year-old skull of a Peruvian child who suffered from scurvy. You want to dig deeper, to learn more, to tap into the passions of the people who found it, donated it, and carefully tucked it away for posterity to find again.

Lost in the Museum is about the thrill of discovering these vast storehouses of stories just waiting to be told. These lush collections open doors to fascinating personalities and to the idiosyncrasies of the places where their possessions are interred. They survive as memorials to the heritage and promise of our society. They stand ready to enthrall our children and our children's children with the new questions they will certainly bring to the long-buried stuff.

JOHN JAMES
AUDUBON'S BIRDS

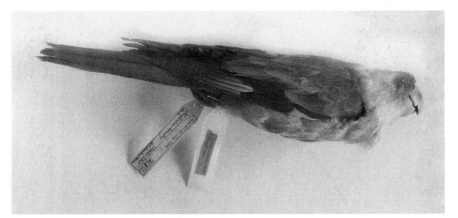

Carolina Parakeet
© Doug Wechsler/VIREO-ANSP

JOHN JAMES AUDUBON'S BIRDS

Academy of Natural Sciences

"Here's something that might interest you," said Dr. Nate Rice, collections manager for ornithology at the Academy of Natural Sciences. Nate was leading me down the banks of cabinets lining the fourth-floor storage crypt; he stopped in front of one, and pulled out a shallow drawer.

Four birds, carefully placed end to end, lined the drawer. These weren't the life-like taxidermied birds that are the common fare of natural history museums like the Academy of Natural Sciences. These birds lay on their sides, clearly dead. Though more than 150 years old, they gleamed with color, with bright orange heads, yellow shoulders, and lime-green breasts. Each had a small paper tag tied to one of its talons.

"These are Audubon's birds," Nate said with a hint of awe in his voice. I gave him a quizzical look. "You remember John James Audubon, don't you, America's most celebrated bird artist? These Carolina parakeets are the actual birds he painted for *Birds of America*, his landmark book. In fact, the Academy's collections hold 225 specimens of birds that Audubon collected as models for his illustrations."

Audubon's actual birds?

I had just been appointed executive director of the Atwater Kent Museum when the Academy's president invited me to meet his curators and to take a behind-the-scenes tour. I arrived early to walk the two vast floors of public galleries, past displays of rocks, bones, shells, and dioramas of animals posed in their natural habitats. Stuffed caribou grazed on dried brown brush in front of a backdrop of pines and mountains; a bored moose stared out from his glass window; a stuffed, snarling polar bear stood protecting his prey, a stuffed, dead seal. The animals looked tired and forlorn. Neglected. Left to stand in their cases for seventy years with little more than an occasional dusting.

Nothing I saw on display that day prepared me for Audubon's birds and the other wonders I found behind closed doors. Audubon's Carolina parakeets *are* natural science. Don't these birds deserve to be put out for all to see? Don't they deserve much more than burial in a storage drawer protected from actual dust but sentenced to the dustbin of science? Don't they deserve a featured spot in the Academy's exhibition gallery, along with the man who shot and painted them?

The Academy of Natural Sciences is set on Benjamin Franklin Parkway in the heart of Philadelphia's museum district. It's much more than meets the eye, the oldest natural history institution in the Western Hemisphere. It owns the bones of a giant ground sloth donated by Thomas Jefferson; the only remaining fossils collected by Lewis and Clark; the skeleton of Bolivar, the famous gorilla who once charmed visitors at the Philadelphia Zoo; and a couple of drawers of tropical beetles the size of small mice. It's the home of generations of seminal scientists: Thomas Say, known as "the Father of Entomology," Admiral Robert E. Peary, famed explorer of the North Pole; Ruth Patrick, environmental pioneer and founder of the Academy's own Patrick Center for Environmental Research. It holds hundreds of thousands of "type specimens," each the singular and special specimen that defines a species of flora or fauna. But you wouldn't know it walking through the galleries. The Academy that the Academy presents to its visitors is not nearly as compelling as the Academy it keeps hidden. While longtime locals carry sweet memories of the Academy from their childhood, from the perspective of many others, the place is upside down.

Audubon's gorgeous and secret birds haunted me. They symbolized the toughest challenge I faced as a museum director: how to use our limited funds to serve the public and preserve the collections. The 80,000 items owned by the Atwater Kent paled next to the Academy's specimens: its 2 million plants, 2 million insects, 2.5 million fish, 10 million shells, and specimens of 80 percent of the world's bird species.

And the Academy was even more complicated than the Atwater Kent. It's more than a museum, more than a treasure house of biodiversity; it's a living, breathing center of scientific research. Scientists from all over the world come here to study its historic collections, and scientists from the Academy travel worldwide to harvest specimens and conduct environmental studies. I hadn't had much direct experience with the scholarly use of collections since graduate school. Only a handful of scholars ever came by the Atwater Kent Museum, since historians seldom draw on museum collections for their research. But scientists do. Specimens are the stuff of scientific research. The expense of ongoing science plus the mammoth cost of caring for this mammoth collection adds up to a whole lot of money. Were finances the reason that the Academy of Natural Sciences showed the public so little of what makes it special?

Because finances are so central to museums, let me explain a bit about how they work. Museums need money, lots of it. You'll seldom meet a museum director who will say there's enough money to do the job right. Of course that's true: every successful director, whether it's of the Metropolitan Museum of Art or the tiny historic house down the street, spends at least three-quarters of his or her time on money: raising it or juggling it to make ends meet. But it's not the whole story. Raising and spending money is all about priorities. Funding sources are available for just about anything museums need: there are tens of thousands of foundations, countless corporate givers, grant programs at every level of government, and many, many rich people. Of course, it takes considerable time, tenacity, and charm to locate the right sources and persuade them to donate their money. But if you follow the money, you'll find the priorities. You'll see what's important to an organization.

As a seasoned fund-raiser, I knew how to find the money. As a new museum director, the challenge was learning what to raise it for. The tough question was how to reconcile the often competing priorities that lay at the heart of the Atwater Kent Museum, the Academy of Natural Sciences, and in fact, all museums. Would Audubon's birds reveal the answer?

I spent a lot of time at the Academy of Natural Sciences over the next few years, touring the basement and attic storerooms, the library, and the archives to see what the public never gets to see, the many items once owned by John James Audubon. I interviewed the three consecutive presidents and a number of the staff, asking them all the same question: why doesn't the Academy have a permanent exhibit about John James Audubon?

In the library, the librarian proudly showed me the one Audubon item the public can see, an original edition of *Birds of America*, one of the few that remain in the hands of their original owners. The historian, an expert on Audubon, explained that the Academy had staged its last major exhibit in 1934, but some Audubon items were brought out on occasion, most recently in 2000 for a temporary show. The exhibits director said that he'd love to create a permanent exhibit about Audubon but it would cost millions that the Academy didn't have. A scientist told me that it was more important to spend money on special steel storage cases to keep the birds from rotting. The three presidents told me that an exhibit about Audubon was included in the new strategic plan, but they weren't sure when it would be possible.

Everyone had reasons, very good reasons, why Audubon's beloved birds remained in their drawer. But I began to fantasize about a permanent exhibit about America's most beloved bird artist that would excavate his possessions from their snug crypts and reveal his connections to art, natural science, and to the Academy itself.

John James Audubon was a self-taught naturalist with a knack for self-promotion. From childhood on, he was possessed by birds—shooting them, stuffing them, studying them, suspending them on wires, and painting them again and again and again. Born in 1785 to a French sea captain and his French mistress in what is now Haiti, Audubon spent his childhood in France, where he received a minimal education. Audubon's father was the first in a long line of family and friends who attempted to curb Audubon's peculiar predilection and direct him toward more practical employment. In 1803 Audubon *pere* sent Audubon *fils* across the ocean to learn how to manage the farm the family owned in Chester County, near Philadelphia.

Soon the young Frenchman met Lucy Bakewell, the daughter of a prosperous neighbor, who became the love of his life and his stalwart through the many trials ahead. To win the hand of his beloved Lucy, young John James needed to prove his worth. In 1806 he returned to France to seek help. Audubon's father and a friend of the father, who also had a son, agreed to bankroll the two young men in business. After a few false starts, Audubon and his partner established a store in the new settlement of Louisville, Kentucky. Lucy came along as the new Mrs. Audubon.

But soon the lure of America's rich wilderness beckoned. Instead of minding the store, Audubon escaped to the woods. He filled his rifle with shot, killed birds by the dozens, and selected out the best specimen. He cut open the breast, pealed the skin back, removed the bones, muscles, organs, and fat, replaced them with fiber stuffing, and preserved the birds with arsenic. Then he hung them on wires and spent hours teaching himself how to capture their images on paper.

In 1820, after a series of failed businesses, John James and the ever faithful Lucy faced the facts: Audubon's true calling was as a painter of birds. He set off to find them in the American wilderness, leaving his wife and two small sons behind to live off the kindness of friends and family, augmented by the few dollars Lucy earned as a tutor in the homes of the wealthy.

While the life of a naturalist painter was more suited to the educated rich than the unschooled poor, Audubon chose the right moment to pursue his dream. The early 1800s were the era of great discovery, when America was teaching itself its own natural science. The Academy of Natural Sciences was epicenter, the only natural history museum in the Americas. Its own Alexander Wilson was the preeminent bird scientist; his graphic depiction of 315 bird species and the accompanying scientific essays earned him the title "the Father of American Ornithology." Audubon had met Wilson briefly in 1810 and had seen two volumes of his work. More than anything else, John James Audubon wanted to be part of this world of science. His ticket of admission would be the first comprehensive collection of all of America's birds, rendered life-size and anatomically correct, and with a narrative accompaniment that would top Wilson's.

After four years of rigorous travel and painting, Audubon came to the Academy and proudly presented his portfolio. Unfortunately, the tactless young naturalist began in the worst possible way; he criticized the work of the recently deceased Alexander Wilson, thus incurring the enmity of Wilson's greatest admirer, the Academy's vice president, George Ord. When Audubon failed to secure an American publisher for his work, he caught a boat to Great Britain. There, he was embraced as the quintessential American woodsman, a romantic figure in the loose clothing and long, flowing hair of the frontiersman. By the time he returned to the United States in 1829, Audubon had secured support, subscribers, and skilled engravers to transform his images into *Birds of America*. A plaster cast in the Academy's rare book room shows Audubon's handsome face; he was a charmer.

A massive effort like *Birds of America* would have exhausted anyone with less grit: its scale stands as testimony to his unbridled optimism. Audubon decided that his birds needed to be shown as big as life, engraved and hand-tinted on the largest and most expensive paper available: double elephant size, 27½ × 39½ inches.

Audubon's plan was to secure subscribers for the entire book, to publish its pictures in sets of five, and to collect funds upon delivery of each set. Only the wealthiest individuals and institutions could afford the enormous cost of *Birds of America*, so Audubon set out to sell the subscriptions himself—one by one.

Thus began Audubon's second extended career, as a salesman. The rest of his life would be shared between the woodlands of his heart and the salons of the rich and famous. On each trip to Europe, he spent his days collecting the payment due from his subscribers and securing new ones, accumulating enough money to publish the next set of prints. He then traveled back to the United States to shoot, stuff, and paint more birds and enlist more customers. In 1838, after twelve long years, 435 bird pictures—thirty-five more than originally envisioned—had been printed, and *Birds of America* was finally finished.

Audubon was a one-man publishing powerhouse. Not only did he find the birds, paint the pictures, oversee the printing, and sell the subscriptions, but by the time of his death in 1851, he had authored a five-volume *Ornithological Biography* to provide scientific background to *Birds of America*; a smaller American edition of his *Birds*; and a wholly new folio on double elephant-size paper, *Viviparous Quadrupeds*, an illustrated compendium of American mammals that bear their young alive. A copy of *Viviparous Quadrupeds* is kept in the library of the Academy of Natural Sciences; two *Sciurus niger*—fox squirrels—featured in the book are stored in the basement.

Audubon's fieldwork took him throughout the Mid-Atlantic, south as far as the Florida Keys, as far southwest as Galveston, Texas, and north into Labrador; the original copperplate for the Labrador falcon is in the

Academy's rare book room. He traveled in every kind of weather on every possible type of conveyance. Along the way, Audubon had many assignments as a drawing tutor, portrait painter, and specimen harvester, as well as elegant dinners with European royalty and American intelligentsia, perhaps a couple of love affairs, and some narrow escapes from creditors. But ever the woodsman, John James's happiest hours were spent at remote wilderness campfires, swapping stories with trappers and Indians.

The Carolina parakeets came from his final journey, as verified by the tag on the birds' talons, written in Audubon's delicate script: "Accession Number 136784 *Conuropsis Ludovicianus*, Carolina Parakeets, May 3, 1843. Collected by Audubon and Harris in Kickapoo country along the Mo.R."

According to his journal, on May 3, 1843, Audubon had just passed Fort Leavenworth, Kansas, the gateway to Indian Territory. Perhaps the Carolina parakeets were among the land and water birds he saw "sailing in marvelous variety after a thunderstorm." At age fifty-eight he remained fit enough to tromp as many as thirty-five miles a day in all kinds of weather. After harvesting the parakeets, he returned home to Lucy, to spend his remaining years in comfort.

John James Audubon eventually received mountains of praise and many distinguished appointments. Perhaps the one that meant the most was his election as corresponding member of the great Academy of Natural Sciences. Though membership votes to the Academy were kept secret, it appears likely that George Ord, Audubon's nemesis, blackballed him twice, belittling his sketches as absurd, fanciful, and pretentious. Nevertheless, by 1831 there was no denying that *Birds of America* was the nation's preeminent ornithological work. Audubon's nomination for corresponding membership, dated 1831 and stored in the archives, documents his acceptance into the Academy's august membership. From the appointment, Audubon gained the scientific standing he needed to sell more books and the access he required to valuable specimens. The Academy of Natural Sciences gained a connection to America's most beloved bird artist that continues to this day.

Audubon was not the most skilled of researchers: his writings are more useful for their engaging description of people, places, and events than for their scientific precision. He also failed in his impossible goal of documenting all of America's birds. Nevertheless, *Birds of America* reigns supreme. Audubon was the first to capture the romance of birds in their natural habitats—diving for fish, breaking open eggs, wading in the water, in flight, in fight, and in song. Like Audubon himself, his birds have verve, personality, and style. While the pictures might appear anatomically inaccurate to ornithologists, for the rest of us they speak directly to the human heart.

Audubon's gorgeous Carolina parakeets once filled the skies over a wide sweep of America. They are now extinct. They were shot, often hundreds at a time, by farmers as pests, and by hunters for food and for their feathers to trim ladies' hats. Even in Audubon's time, Carolina parakeets were at risk, a situation he mourned in *Ornithological Biography*. "Our parakeets are very rapidly diminishing in number," he wrote, "and in some districts, where twenty-five years ago they were plentiful, scarcely any are now to be seen."

My obsession with Audubon's birds and the mystery of museum management they symbolized outlasted my tenure at the Atwater Kent Museum. I purchased a copy of *Birds of America*; my favorite was Plate #5, "Carolina Parakeet," which showed seven birds perched on a cocklebur bush, grooming, flying, and preparing to pluck the prickly burs to get to the seed inside. They seemed to smile through the centuries as they showed off their luxurious feathers.

Pondering the drab dioramas in the Academy's galleries, I traveled to New York City to the American Museum of Natural History, one of the grandest of them all. Its stuffed animals were neither lost nor forlorn; in fact, they were as engaging and elegant as mannequins in swank department store windows circa 1930. I stood in awe before the *Spectrum of Life*, a wall one hundred feet long that featured more than 1,500 specimens and models—from microorganisms and mammals to fungi and fish—organized by ever increasing biological complexity to illustrate 3.5 billion years of evolution. I was surprised to learn that the current director of exhibits at the Academy of Natural Sciences had worked at the American Museum of Natural History and been the wall's creator.

That trip revealed the exciting possibilities inherent in dioramas and other natural history exhibits. I realized that the Academy of Natural Sciences had all the ingredients for the Audubon exhibit of my dreams: a large cache of his possessions, a talented exhibition designer, a leading Audubon scholar, and a group of curators who knew their birds and bones. So why was this exhibit nothing more than another item in the Academy's strategic plan? Why weren't they out raising funds for it?

The Academy of Natural Sciences said its priority was scientific research. It was time to return to learn more about the science.

On this visit, Leo Joseph greeted me. Head of the ornithology department, Leo was a fit, forty-ish man with curly hair who spoke with the lilt of his Australian home. He led me up the three flights of stairs to the silent, secured storage room on the fourth floor. It's about a city block long, ringed with offices where scientists were busy at work. The center of the space was banked with nine-foot-high steel cabinets coated with specially baked enamel, which were used for compact storage of specimens. Each cabinet was stacked with drawers; each drawer held rows of bugs, birds, and other fauna.

Leo Joseph turned a crank at the end of one of the cabinets, opening a pathway between two rows. He pulled out a drawer. There were Audubon's dead birds. It was like visiting old friends.

"Audubon was operating at a time when brand new species were being discovered all the time. Naturalists would discover a species and collect a few specimens preserved as dried skins, but today we collect tissue samples for DNA analysis and other kinds of specimens, not just dried skins," said Leo.

"Much of my work is spent studying the birds in the Academy's collections," he continued. "Museum people are interested in evolution and classification; classification is the base of the pyramid of knowledge. You begin with the type specimen, the single specimen that defines our understanding of what a particular species is. These are special treasures in museums. Then you collect more specimens to understand variation within and between species to see how the birds have evolved."

"There are a lot of birds here," I said. "Why does the Academy need more?"

Leo looked at me quizzically. "We are primarily a research institution, and as a research institution we continue to collect. In fact, we need to collect many specimens of the same bird to show all the different levels of variation: their sex, their age, migrant versus non-migrant, different appearances, location. I'm working on an exhibit about John Gould, an Englishman who was a contemporary of Audubon. The Academy owns the lion's share of Gould's Australian birds. It was the first collection the Academy purchased, in 1848. I just came back from a collecting trip in Australia. Let's go take a look."

Leo led me down an alley between more storage cabinets to an over-sized, humming, walk-in freezer. "The newly obtained specimens from my Australian trip are kept here before being placed in the collection," he said, unlocking the massive door and letting a shock of frigid air escape. "The freezer's kept at minus twenty degrees Celsius. It's for freezing and killing any unwanted bugs that might have hitched a ride with packing materials used with incoming specimens. That way new specimens don't contaminate our collection." He reached into a four-foot drum of liquid nitrogen and pulled out a ladle with a scoop on the end. In it were five tiny vials with murky gray gunk on the bottom. "These are cryofrozen tissue samples from the Australian birds," he said. "The cylinder is filled with liquid nitrogen until the specimens make it back here, and then we store them in a freezer at minus eighty degrees Celsius, to preserve them forever."

"Why do you need to preserve the innards?" I asked.

"Ah," said Leo smiling. "That's where we've advanced since Audubon's time. The tissue samples contain DNA, and with the DNA, we can actually trace the path of evolution. Recently, another scientist used bird feathers to prove the existence of global warming. He compared the kinds of carbon isotopes in feathers from birds collected one hundred years ago in Alaska to feathers from the same birds he harvested there recently, and found a change in carbon in today's birds that reflects global warming."

"It's clear why it's important to keep specimens from the past if the birds exist today," I said. "But why save Audubon's Carolina parakeets? You can't compare them with today's Carolina parakeets since they're extinct."

Leo stopped for a minute, considering the question. "Why save Audubon's birds? Audubon's birds are our heritage, all the evidence we've got to pass along to future generations. They're the only record of the only parrot found in the United States. If we want to understand parrots fully, we've got to begin with extinct species.

"There's something else," he said frowning. "We are responsible for the bird's loss. Hell, we should be hanging our heads in shame, not throwing them out. Our collection is just bristling with knowledge waiting to be tapped, part of a worldwide collection, a meta-collection of historic specimens. Although many researchers still have to come here to study our specimens, many needs of scientists, graduate students, and even book illustrators from all over the world can be met by electronic access, by computer."

I finally got it. What looks to the public like a natural history museum is actually a gigantic research center with a museum tacked on, a museum with dated exhibits that evidence some considerable benign neglect.

Founded by an apothecary, a dentist, and four of their friends in 1812, the Academy of Natural Sciences was a first: dedicated to "the acquirements, increase, simplification, and diffusion of natural knowledge." In keeping with the origins of early science museums, these gentlemen scientists essentially brought their personal collections and books to a central location. Soon the institution began attracting the cream of early America's naturalists, who also brought their specimens: brilliant butterflies collected by Titian Ramsay Peale, animals from David Livingston's African journeys, the jaw of an extinct fish from Thomas Jefferson, the only fossil vertebrae remains from Lewis and Clark's expedition. Within five years, the institution began publishing the *Journal of the Academy of Natural Science* so naturalists worldwide could share knowledge.

The Academy sort of backed into its museum. In 1828, in response to popular demand, it opened the doors to its members and their friends every Tuesday and Thursday afternoon. Large crowds began arriving around the time of the Civil War, to admire the first nearly complete dinosaur skeleton ever found, excavated just a few short miles away, in Haddonfield, New Jersey. Over 3,000 visitors showed up every week. The public loved it; the scientists did not. As early as 1861, curators were complaining that the "movements of the crowds of visitors give rise to clouds of dust, which penetrates the cases and obscures the specimens." When research drives the mission, the public can become an inconvenience.

While no one at the Academy today would say that the public is an inconvenience, it's nevertheless true that science is the priority. The same genus of science aficionados who founded the place almost 200 years ago continues to dominate the board. Perhaps most telling is capital investment in the museum. The largest recent renovation was

Dinosaur Hall, installed in 1986. There's a new space where children handle live animals and a live butterfly habitat. Nevertheless, for visitors, the overall experience is more akin to a mausoleum of rocks, flora, and fauna than a living center of cutting-edge science. That's a problem, especially if you're competing for the public's attention—and dollars.

"Dinosaur Museum Is Itself Threatened," read the headline of a front-page story in the *Philadelphia Inquirer* in December 2005. The article went on to relate the Academy's chronic and escalating problems with money. None of its three divisions generated enough to support its work. For years, the board had met the annual deficit by taking small nibbles and large bites out of the corpus of its endowment, which in 2005 totaled $56 million. The scientific staff was depleted; Leo Joseph, expert bird curator, had returned to his native Australia.

In October 2006, another newspaper story reported that the Academy's board had voted to sell more than 15,000 minerals and gems that had never been displayed and to use the proceeds to support the library. Between 1998, when I first visited Audubon's birds, and 2006 when the second story appeared, three able presidents with unusually brief tenures had led the place. When you see this kind of turnover, something serious is going on.

It often takes a crisis to force an institution to face up to long-simmering problems. This one may spur the board to think long and hard about a new direction, since the one they've been following for decades no longer works. The central question is: what makes the Academy special, what makes it unique and worth supporting?

Perhaps John James Audubon's remarkable life, his dead birds, stuffed squirrels, life mask, artwork, books, and documents will point the way to the answer. Perhaps they will inspire the Academy to bring downstairs, into the galleries, the fascinating specimens and cutting-edge research hidden upstairs, behind closed doors.

It would take many years, millions of dollars, and a profound shift in institutional priorities to achieve this dream. But when you're the oldest natural history museum in the Western Hemisphere, it might be worth the effort. Audubon's birds are emblematic of what makes the Academy memorable: its almost two-century-long engagement with the natural wonders of the nation and the world.

BLASCHKA
SEA ANIMALS

"A member of the species Siphonophora," by Leopold and Rudolf Blaschka
Courtesy of the Carnegie Museum of Art, Pittsburgh,
transferred from the Carnegie Museum of Natural History

BLASCHKA SEA ANIMALS

Carnegie Museums of Pittsburgh

Six mysterious objects lined a display case in a half-empty gallery in the Carnegie Museum of Art. Five somewhat resembled things they clearly were not: the padded base of a dress hanger, a lampshade, an urn, a shrimp, and four sherry glasses made of curved icicles. The sixth was very weird; something that looked like a rope snaked down to a lozenge and a sphere and up to two bulbs with spiny spikes at their tops. The objects were made of clear and colored glass and featured delicate filaments, fans of feathers, and sinuous tentacles. Ranging in height from three to about eight inches, each was suspended by glass straws over a clear glass base.

These mysterious objects were actually educational models of sea invertebrates. The Carnegie Museum of Natural History had purchased them around 1900, displayed them for decades as part of scientific exhibits, and then stored them away when they became obsolete. Recently rediscovered, they were now featured in an exhibit entitled *Fierce Friends: Artists and Animals, 1750–1900* at the Carnegie Museum of Art. How they morphed from science to art reveals the special character of their home, the Carnegie Museums of Pittsburgh, and its central role in the life of the city.

The main building of the Carnegie Museums of Pittsburgh used to be called the Carnegie Institute. Its sprawling structure is located in the

Oakland section of the city, a couple of blocks from my childhood home. Pittsburgh in the 1950s held only a handful of options for a young girl with a budding appetite for culture, so I'd spent countless hours happily meandering through its halls. I'd attended story readings in the children's room of the Carnegie Library and concerts in the Music Hall. I'd gone on countless class trips to visit the dinosaurs at the natural history museum and the art museum's biannual *International* exhibitions. For years, I'd spent Saturday mornings sketching with thick black crayons on grainy newsprint with a couple of hundred other kids judged to have talent by their school art teachers. Now I was back to see how the Carnegie of my memories matched up with the place today.

The Carnegie is an everything-in-the-world museum, a type common to many mid-sized midwestern cities, where different types of museums share the same roof. The one in Pittsburgh was created whole cloth by a single vision: that of Andrew Carnegie, America's first great philanthropist. Born in Dunfermline, Scotland, in 1835, he embodied the can-do spirit of American enterprise. Andrew Carnegie was a complicated man: controlling and paternalistic, tough and generous, agnostic, Darwinian, an advocate for world peace, and something of a mama's boy who did not marry until he was fifty-two and his mother was snug in her grave.

Carnegie saw the future of Pittsburgh at the cusp of its transformation from dirty, work-a-day factory town to great metropolis. Scores of his company's partners and managers became overnight millionaires in 1901 when he sold the Carnegie Company to the newly created United Steel Corporation for $250 million—over $5.7 billion in today's dollars. The city was ready for culture. And Carnegie was ready to deliver it. After he made his millions, he spent the rest of his life giving them away. In the *Gospel of Wealth*, his 1889 manifesto on philanthropy, he laid out his philosophy:

> This, then, is held to be the duty of the man of wealth: first, to set an example of modest unostentatious living, shunning display; to provide moderately for the legitimate wants of those dependent upon him; and, after doing so, to consider all surplus revenues which come to him simply as trust funds which he is strictly bound as a matter of duty to administer in the manner which, in his judgment, is best calculated to produce the most beneficial results for the community.

The *Gospel of Wealth* was nothing less than revolutionary; it stunned his contemporaries. But over time, it inspired generations of millionaires and billionaires—up to Bill Gates and Warren Buffet—to live modestly and invest the bulk of their fortunes in serving society.

In Carnegie's time, many reformers were concerned with helping the poorest, the most destitute. Carnegie had a different point of view; he believed in helping those he called the "swimming one-tenth," those who didn't just float along, but wanted to better themselves, their prospects. He wanted to help those who made the effort to help themselves.

Although Andrew Carnegie's formal schooling ended at age thirteen when his family left Scotland for America, he was a voracious reader and strong believer in the self-education that was so central to his life. The Carnegie is infused with this spirit.

Carnegie's initial idea was to build a grand free library for Pittsburgh, and in 1881 he offered the mayor $250,000 to erect one if the city would provide the land and annual tax support for its maintenance. The mayor could not accept Carnegie's offer, because the laws of Pennsylvania did not allow taxes to be used to maintain a library. After the Pennsylvania legislature changed the law, Pittsburgh quickly requested that Carnegie renew the offer. By that time, the philanthropist had hit on a grander scheme, a great palace of culture that would include a free library, a music hall, a great museum, and an art institute. In 1890, he put $1 million on the table, if the city provided land and $40,000 per year for maintenance. Pittsburgh's mayor promptly agreed.

The day in August of 2006 I returned to Pittsburgh to see the Carnegie's mysterious glass objects, I was greeted by a gray sky threatening rain. I walked up the wide steps of the original 1895 building, which houses the Carnegie Music Hall and the main branch of the Carnegie Library. College students recently returned from summer vacation were consulting librarians who sat at desks below frosted glass signs that read "Ask a librarian" and "Can I help you?" People were typing busily at computer stations, roaming through the open stacks, and reading books in a bamboo-filled atrium. In the children's room, parents and toddlers were reading on a comfy sofa and at child-height tables painted bright red and yellow. Wide windows framed Pittsburgh's landscape, the lawn strewn with brown leaves, the orderly row of parked cars, the wide drive beyond.

Through a wooden doorway at the east end of the library, I entered the great Hall of Architecture located in the building's 1907 addition.

The hall houses the nation's largest surviving collection of architectural plaster casts. I stood in child-like wonder before the portal of the north transept of the Cathedral of Sainte-Andre at Bordeaux, the Choregic Monument of Lysicrates, the model of the Parthenon, one-twentieth the size of the original. Along a wall were plaster casts of the beloved Apollo Belvedere, Venus de Milo, and famed Discus Thrower by Myron. Andrew Carnegie had purchased the entire lot, believing that ordinary Pittsburghers deserved to experience European masterpieces, then only available to those wealthy enough to travel abroad. He insisted the nudes be draped so as not to offend. And, to make them available to working people, the galleries were free and open Herculean hours: from 10 a.m. to 10 p.m. six days per week and from 2 p.m. to 6 p.m. on Sundays.

The Carnegie Library and Institute was not Andrew Carnegie's first philanthropic gesture, but certainly it was his grandest at the time. Like his massive steel mills, everything in his palace of culture was housed under the same roof, to eliminate management overlaps and to expedite efficiency. He wanted to be consulted on every detail, from the architectural design to the names of the artists, scientists, and authors carved in stone on the entablature. He added new elements, rearranging things and contributing money as he went along. In 1896, he donated $1 million to form the Carnegie Institute's Department of Fine Arts and Museum. Four years later, he added another $1 million for a technical school, which was managed by the board of the Carnegie Institute; this eventually became Carnegie Mellon University. Over time, the Department of Fine Arts evolved into the Carnegie Museum of Art and the Department of the Museum became the Carnegie Museum of Natural History.

Next to the Hall of Architecture was the Museum of Natural History, Andrew Carnegie's special love: his enthusiasm for American science made it the "home of the dinosaurs" when he helped underwrite the earliest excavations in what now is Dinosaur National Monument in Utah. Behind a wall of glass in the PaleoLab, I watched as white-coated technicians vacuumed dust off dinosaur bones. Across the way, a major renovation was underway in Dinosaur Hall, the star attraction. I entered a gallery: "The Pleistocene Epoch, 1.8 million years ago to 10,000 years ago," read the sign. Along the wall paraded the ancient skeletons I remembered from my youth: the *Archaeotherium mortoni*, the giant pig; the *Merychyus minimus,* an oreodonte, a cross between a sheep and a pig about the size of a pet cat; three *Stenomylus,* the species of small gazelle-like camels, as delicate as greyhounds.

The hallway outside the Carnegie Museum of Natural History is tiled in rhythmic squares of color. I walked down the hall and crossed the threshold into the cool gray granite of the Carnegie Museum of Art. In front of the restaurant, Jean Dubuffet's wall-sized sculpture *The Free Exchange* gleamed in red, white, and black, its acrylic-on-epoxy paper-doll-like figures slowly rising and falling to the hum of its engine. I asked the guard to call Louise Lippincott, chief curator and curator of fine arts of the Carnegie Museums of Pittsburgh.

"What a pleasure to spend time actually discussing art," said Louise Lippincott, smiling as she greeted me in her cluttered, light-filled office. With salt-and-pepper, shoulder-length hair, she was wearing rimless glasses, a long-sleeved jersey with an Indian motif, and black slacks. "Let's go see the Blaschka sea animals. *Fierce Friends* is being dismantled, but they're still on display."

Lippincott led me to an elevator, from which we exited on the main floor of the art museum and walked into the Heinz Galleries, which are reserved for special exhibitions. *Fierce Friends* had just closed to the public after a five-month run. Co-produced by the Van Gogh Museum of Amsterdam and the Carnegie Museum of Art, the interdisciplinary show was the first serious, full-scale examination of the subject of animals in art. The first to incorporate scientific materials and concepts, it combined ninety-five artistic masterpieces drawn from important U.S. and European collections with animal specimens, skeletons, and other scientific material. It was perfect for the Carnegie, where art and science have happily co-existed for over one hundred years.

The walls of the Heinz Galleries were painted in soft shades of blue and green to set off the vibrant oil paintings, illustrations, and text panels. A couple of technicians were carefully removing objects from the rough plywood display cases and placing them on carts. Across the room stood a case about seven feet tall with light pouring over stuffed bird carcasses, displayed as elegantly as art objects. "These are the same birds portrayed in John James Audubon's *Birds of America,* and on this set of Meissen," Lippincott said, pointing first to the over-sized books that lay open in a case, and then to the china plates and serving pieces displayed nearby.

"Here are our Blaschkas," she said, leading me to the six glass objects. No one has ever been able to duplicate them."

I read the labels next to each one. The padded dress hanger was actually a glass replica of a sea worm with an anemone on top. The fan of four icicle sherry glasses was a species of glass sponge. The urn with tentacles was a hydra; the fringed lampshade and weird item with the rope, lozenge, and sphere were species of jellyfish. The spiny shrimp was a *Copepoda*, whatever that was.

The objects were the products—really the creations—of two extraordinary glass artists, Leopold and Rudolf Blaschka, father and son, who lived and worked in mid-nineteenth-century Bohemia. Glass making was the family business; as early as the fifteenth century, Blaschkas were fashioning decorative items and jewelry out of glass. The father, Leopold, was born in 1822, and although he showed an early aptitude for painting, his own father had a more practical future in mind, so Leopold joined the family firm. Within a couple of years, Leopold's wife and father died, and the despondent young man decided to make his way in America. On the voyage over, his ship was becalmed for two weeks. Leopold spent the time trawling for jellyfish and drawing them from life. This was his first encounter with sea invertebrates; it inspired his artistry and revolutionized the field of natural history models.

After a couple of months in the United States, Leopold Blaschka returned home, remarried, and established a workshop in the home of his new father-in-law. In his free time, Leopold began to experiment with glass replicas of natural forms, beginning with the exotic orchids in the greenhouses of Prince Camille de Rohan. In 1863, one hundred models of fifty species of orchids were exhibited in the Royal Botanical Garden in Dresden. An Englishman who saw them invited Blaschka to test this glass artist's talent on marine invertebrates.

The mid-nineteenth century was an explosion of new knowledge, a time when scientists spanned the world collecting rare flora and fauna. Some of the specimens ended up in the new museums just being built and in older ones recently opened to the public. Many groups of animals—birds, mammals, reptiles, and fish—could be skinned, stuffed, and placed on display. But soft-bodied creatures, marine invertebrates like sea anemones and jellyfish, proved more problematic. When pickled and placed in jars, they quickly lost their shape and color. How to capture their feathery gills and luminous hues and present them for public view?

Leopold put his talent to the task. He began by studying scientific illustrations of marine invertebrates, spending hours trying to replicate them in glass. Things did not go well at first: not only was it difficult to translate from two-dimensional pictures to three-dimensional objects, but many of the illustrations lacked scientific accuracy. Nevertheless, Leopold was captivated by the challenge. By 1871 he had produced some 300 different models of worms, echinoderms, mollusks, and jellyfish ready for sale as *objets d'art* to wealthy collectors and as educational models to universities and natural history museums.

Soon Leopold's young son, Rudolf, joined his father in finding new illustrations in the great national history library of the Imperial Academy Leopoldina in Dresden. At the same time, the Blaschka factory continued to produce glass jewelry, fans, and artificial eyes. When the South Kensington Museum in London ordered two complete collections of invertebrate models in 1876, father and son put the decorative glass business aside to devote all of their time to scientific model making.

The next year, the Blaschkas met Professor Ernst Haeckel, a prominent zoologist at the University of Jena in Germany, who shared their interest in marine invertebrates. Haeckel's work on invertebrates was the first to follow Charles Darwin's theory of evolution.

The Carnegie's mysterious models of marine life originated with Professor Haeckel and can be found among the one hundred illustrations in his most celebrated book, *Kunstsformen der Natur* (*Art Forms in Nature*). Wildly popular at the time, Haeckel's meticulously detailed renderings reveal both his taxonomic acumen and aesthetic sensibilities. He believed in the perfection of nature and that perfection was symmetry, so his sea creatures bridged science and art in their curving forms and remarkable symmetry—perhaps more symmetry than was scientifically accurate. Nevertheless, Haeckel's work inspired generations of scientists as well as the Blaschkas, father and son. The professor's highly ornamental images of jellyfish, mollusks, and other invertebrates were reproduced in scientific encyclopedias and displayed as art in the stylish Art Nouveau homes of his contemporaries.

Within a couple of years the Blaschkas were ordering live specimens of marine invertebrates and placing them in their recently purchased seawater aquarium. By 1888 the catalog produced by their agent in the United States listed 700 models, many considerably improved by the glass artists' encounters with living specimens and their new scientist colleague.

Take for example the *Siphonophorae*, or hydra, featured in *Fierce Friends*. It looked like an orange vase with a fluted base and a cap-like top surrounded by a halo of blue tentacles. I studied it closely, its tentacles undulating in an invisible sea.

"Now, look at the illustration," said Louise Lippincott, handing me a photocopy of a page from *Art Forms in Nature*. "It's identical. During *Fierce Friends* we posted pages from Haeckel's book next to the Blaschkas to show the connection."

Nearby was the *Copepoda*, an elegant, shrimp-like creature with a tail of red feathers and long tentacles waving from its head. Feathery filaments flowed out from the tentacles. The Blaschkas achieved their life-like effect by combining various forms of glass: blown glass, lamp-worked, and modeled; glass that was clear, colored during the manufacturing process, enameled, and painted on when the figures were cold. Some elements were directly fused to the figures, others attached with animal glue. To replicate reality, the Blaschkas also employed fine copper wires, wax, and painted paper.

"They're so delicate," I said, admiring the filaments, so fragile a breeze could break them. "How did they survive?"

"Not everything did," said Lippincott. "Some of the filaments broke off. We replaced them, but in an ethically responsible way."

"Ethically responsible?" I repeated.

"Yes, that's a basic tenet of restoration. When artwork is restored, you use material that's physically different from the original but aesthetically similar, and so the new material can be removed in the future. It's the difference between restoration and fakery. But we were lucky. No one much had touched them for almost eighty years. With fragile objects like these, nothing beats neglect."

"What does it take to create a show like this?" I asked, looking around.

Louise Lippincott sighed. "It's quite a long process. This one took about five years. The Carnegie had recently collaborated with the Van Gogh Museum on a very successful interdisciplinary exhibition about light in the industrial age and we were looking for another topic that combined art and science. Andreas Blühm, my counterpart at the Van Gogh Museum, suggested animals. It was a topic of art history that had not been looked at for a long time. It provided the opportunity to balance art and science equally. The Van Gogh wanted to attract local residents; we wanted to show international masterpieces. Animals in art fit all the requirements."

The first challenge was to find the objects, the blockbuster paintings and sculpture they wanted for the show. This kind of research used to take a lot of travel, but today digital images and emails make things much easier. By the second year, the collaborating curators had the main idea and a list of about twenty images to sell the show internally to colleagues and externally to grant sources.

"Did the board of the museum get involved?" I asked.

"Not really," she replied. "We certainly inform the board, but decisions about exhibits are made by the staff."

"What about the budget?" I asked, remembering from my days as a museum director how much exhibits cost, and how tough they are to finance.

"The Van Gogh Museum is a very popular tourist attraction and earns much of its budget from admissions. Raising funds was not an issue there," explained Lippincott. "The Pittsburgh exhibition cost between $1.2 million and $1.3 million and most of it came from local foundations. Because of the success of the *Light* exhibition, raising the funds for *Fierce Friends* was relatively easy, though some of the money came in quite late. The tough part was financing the planning: you have to invest about 10 percent of the overall budget in planning."

Oh yes. I remembered. That up-front investment was the bane of my existence when I was executive director of Atwater Kent. It's a delicate dance to get in the last dollars for the show that's about to open, while simultaneously getting out the grant proposals for the next one in line. And grant proposals take endless work. To convince a foundation or government agency to invest its dollars in your dream exhibit, the proposal that sells it must detail the entire project: the rationale, objects, work plan, staffing, marketing program, and budget. No wonder it took Lippincott and her colleagues two years to assemble the extensive information needed to complete winning grant proposals.

"The next step was to write the book, the catalog, which has to be finished a year before the exhibit opens; the show opened in Amsterdam six months before here," Lippincott continued. "To write the catalog, you need to know what's in the exhibit. So, before work on the catalog could begin, we had to secure permission from museums and other institutions for loans of artwork. As it turned out, three different versions of the exhibition were created: one for the catalog, one for Amsterdam, and one for Pittsburgh. All included the same ninety-five paintings and sculpture, but each presented them in different ways. In Amsterdam, the exhibition was more family-focused; it featured circus and other anthropomorphic animals. Here, we focused on natural history specimens. The show at the Van Gogh displayed about 150 objects, while ours included 300. All of the books, decorative art, and specimens in this gallery come from the Carnegie," she said proudly with a sweep of her hand.

With the objects selected, Blühm and Lippincott began to work on the structure and design of each exhibit. With the Carnegie Museum of Natural History's curatorial staff, Lippincott began to explore how its specimens could move the show. The Van Gogh Museum worked with a natural history museum in Amsterdam; Lippincott just had to walk down the hall.

"Where did the Blaschkas come in?" I asked.

"I knew the Van Gogh was going to present some Blaschka models, but because the objects were so delicate, it was impossible to transport them to Pittsburgh. During a chance conversation in our hallway, I mentioned the Blaschkas and learned that the Natural History Museum had found a stash of them in storage. When Jacques Cousteau perfected the aqualung, and the era of gorgeous full-color underwater photography began, the models became obsolete. Remember, it's a science museum, so it must present current science. Museums don't generally save display materials, but we got lucky. Call Deborah Harding; she's the collections manager in the anthropology department of the Museum of Natural History. She'll fill you in."

"The Blaschka models? That's quite a story," said Deborah Harding when I called. "All of the models had been purchased by the exhibits department around 1900 from Ward's Natural Science Establishment in Rochester, New York—they're still in business—and all were exhibited once upon a time. The jellyfish, shrimp-like guy, and other invertebrates had been part of a display, I think in Paleozoic Hall, until the late 1980s when the hall was renovated. One of our staff members learned they were going to be pitched and rescued them for the anthropology department. The one-cell animals were in 'forty acres,' that's the storage space now used for the Alcoa Foundation Hall of American Indians. They were still in their original display case: someone just moved the entire case into storage sometime in the 1930s. When we found them somewhat late in the game, Louise and her team were thrilled."

"I remember the day that the art people, an art handler and a conservator, came to pick them up from the off-site storage facility," she continued. "The objects are so fragile; the staff had to build special boxes with fitted spaces and pack them in, oh so very carefully. It was the only way to move them between buildings in the back of somebody's car."

So, quite by happenstance, *Fierce Friends* featured an entire exhibit case of the thirty recently rediscovered Blaschkas, the one-cell animals from "forty acres," mounted as if seen through a microscope lens. Visitors found them so intriguing that stools were set up next to the case so people could study the models closely.

"It must have been a challenge, working with natural history curators," I said to Louise Lippincott. "What differences did you find in how natural history and art curators approached their work?"

"The main difference is that art curators don't have to shoot their specimens," she smiled. "But really, our attitudes are the same. We both study objects hard, preserve them well, and present them to the public."

She thought for a moment. "There's another important difference. The public understands the importance of science, so it's willing to support natural history museums. They view art museums differently; we have to justify our existence, our importance. The questions become more frequent in bad economic times, like now when there's a war on, and there are so many pressures for dollars."

Because animal specimens and skeletons were included in the show, there was some concern about the potential for controversy. Evolution is a hot-button issue: in fact, while *Fierce Friends* was in planning, parents in Dover, Pennsylvania, took their school board to court over whether "intelligent design" should be taught in public school. The art museum held focus groups about the controversy in the neighboring town; participants said they didn't care about it.

"So, are the Blaschkas science or are they art?" I asked.

"These are fabulous works of art: the Blaschkas saw themselves as artists; if they considered themselves craftsmen, it was of the most refined sphere," said Lippincott. "They were intimately involved in each piece. But remember, the Blaschkas were in the scientific model-making business. The models were created at the height of the Art Nouveau movement, but the Blaschkas ignored style; their sea creatures still look very much alive, products of nature rather than man-made."

In 1886 the Harvard Botanical Museum hired Leopold and Rudolf Blaschka to create one-of-a-kind glass replicas of its flowers, and soon thereafter the marine-model business ended. Leopold died in 1895; his son continued to work until age eighty-two, three years before his death in 1936.

During the height of their popularity, Blaschka glass invertebrates graced homes, museums, and universities throughout the world. But when fashion changed and science moved on, many were discarded or broken. Only a few remained in American collections, saved—sometimes by accident—in places like Cornell University, the Harvard Museum of Comparative Zoology, the Museum of Science in Boston, the Academy of Natural Sciences in Philadelphia, and the Carnegie. Now they're being pulled out of storage and placed on display, this time as art. In 2002, an art exhibit entitled *Leopold and Rudolf Blaschka: The Glass Aquarium* opened at the Design Museum in London and then traveled to other museums in England, Scotland, Wales, and Germany.

The day after my visit with Lippincott, I returned to walk through the Carnegie Museum of Art. I climbed up the flight of wide granite stairs that float next to a two-story glass wall to the Scaife Galleries, which hold the permanent collection.

Andrew Carnegie was not a collector of fine art, and his tastes ran toward the figurative and didactic. Instead of following the path of Henry Clay Frick, Andrew Mellon, and others who purchased expensive paintings by old masters, the frugal Scotsman decided to save money by investing in the "old masters of tomorrow." In 1896, the Art Gallery became the nation's first contemporary art museum when it launched the first in a series of biannual public exhibitions of living artists. The trustees and director would then decide which two artworks to purchase for the permanent collection. Because they shared Carnegie's conservative tastes, avant-garde and abstract art was excluded until the 1950s. Andrew Carnegie did not provide funds for art acquisition, leaving that to the generosity of his Pittsburgh millionaire friends. That and the original focus on "the old masters of tomorrow" left major gaps in the collection, which later directors worked hard to fill. While the rest of the art world moved forward, the Carnegie meandered a bit behind.

Walking through the permanent galleries, I was struck by how cleverly they were designed. In "European and American Art, 1850–1880," the paintings were displayed in salon style, with gilded-framed paintings hung from waist height almost to the ceiling. Decorative art was added to provide breadth and context. Each gallery was all of a piece, enveloping the visitor; the labels were detailed, thought-provoking. I returned to Louise Lippincott's office to ask about this.

"Oh yes," she said, surprised by the question. "I do have a philosophy about exhibitions. For a museum installation to work, people should be able to walk into an area and get the point without reading the labels. Your argument has to be visual, through the objects themselves. Exhibits are different than books. A book is a flow of words with images attached, or with a picture book, pictures with words attached. In exhibitions, it's all about juxtaposing objects in space. There's a physical difference, a different relationship between the viewer and the object.

"In *Fierce Friends*, Paul Rosenblatt, the space designer, was a real partner, an enormous help in this regard. I played 'paper dolls' for hours, arranging and rearranging photos of the artwork chronologically and thematically," she said, pointing to the pitted board covering a wall in her office. "Paul took one look and came up with a much better way to organize the show."

"What about the labels?" I asked.

"I wrote them myself," she said. "I'm very possessive about content. I do a lot of checking to assure accuracy. Object labels need to say something concrete—but also to relate to the whole world. I think of them as haiku, you know, the Japanese poetry form that calls for seventeen syllables. It takes a lot of concerted effort to write a haiku, to write a really good label, but I enjoy it. I was still writing labels for *Fierce Friends* until six days before the exhibit opened."

Fierce Friends was quite an undertaking. Artwork had to be requested and permissions secured from more than seventy European and American lenders: museums, universities, Queen Elizabeth herself. Each item had to be packed carefully, shipped, received, inspected, hung, and labeled. Five years, multiple grant proposals, $1.3 million.

"After all the work, all the money, the show was only up for five months. Doesn't that make you sad when it closes?" I asked.

"Not really," responded Lippincott. "For me, the fun is putting it all together. Once it's up, the creative thrill is over and I'm deep into the next one."

She reflected for a moment. "But theme shows like *Fierce Friends* do have a lasting impact; the purpose lives on. Other museums will produce interdisciplinary exhibits about science and art. And visitors will remember it as something special. The impact is there, but it's subtle and emerges over time."

Time has been good to the Carnegie. The place I remembered from my youth was a bit provincial, an everything-in-the-world museum where natural history and art shared a roof but little else. What I found on my return was a place alive with visitors and new ideas. As the traditional barriers between art and science have softened, the Carnegie Museums of Pittsburgh is using exhibits like *Light* and *Fierce Friends* to carve a distinctive niche in the cultural world, not as a place meandering behind, but as one on the vanguard of a new merging, a new sensibility.

The Carnegie Museums of Pittsburgh now includes two other museums on Pittsburgh's North Side: the Carnegie Science Center which opened its doors in 1991, and the Andy Warhol Museum which opened in 1994 as a tribute to this Pittsburgh-born artist. More than fifty performing arts, museums, galleries, and historical societies now join them in the rich mix of opportunities available to girls and boys with an appetite for culture.

Leopold and Rudolph Blaschka's display models of marine invertebrates are back in storage, this time in the decorative arts department of the Carnegie Museum of Art. These fabulous sea creatures remind us of Andrew Carnegie's practicality—and prescience—in creating a single palace of culture for separate museums of art and natural history. They reveal the art in science, the science in art, and a new frontier of interdisciplinary exhibitions where the connections between them come clear.

FRANKLIN B.
GOWEN'S BOWL

Franklin B. Gowen's Bowl
Courtesy of the Historical Society of Pennsylvania Collection, Atwater Kent Museum of Philadelphia

FRANKLIN B. GOWEN'S BOWL

Historical Society of Pennsylvania

At first glance the majestic silver bowl appears to be the kind of commemorative item common to most every historical society. It is the kind of trophy Victorian gentlemen gave to one of their own to celebrate a race well run or a magnificent contribution to humankind. What makes this bowl so shocking and provocative is what it celebrates: Franklin Benjamin Gowen's singular achievement of destroying one of America's first industrial labor unions.

Franklin Gowen's bowl—more than thirty-six pounds of intricately worked sterling silver and gold—recalls the bitter battles of early labor organizing, the rise and fall of a gigantic industrial conglomerate, and the power of a single man to control the nation's most prized commodity when coal was king and America was in its Gilded Age. The bowl holds another story, one about a collecting institution that almost imploded when Susan Stitt, its dynamic, seasoned president, forced it to change. A single object can tell a world of stories. This one tells the story of hubris.

The institution is the Historical Society of Pennsylvania, the owner of Franklin Gowen's bowl. In Philadelphia, which boasts more historical societies, sites, and museums than any place in the country, the Historical Society of Pennsylvania is the leader of the pack. Founded in 1824 by Pennsylvania's most distinguished families, the Society has long been known for its vast trove of historical treasures. Among its possessions are the most complete set of papers of Pennsylvania's founder, William Penn; a printer's proof of the Declaration of Independence; a copy of the Emancipation Proclamation; and the first two drafts of the U.S. Constitution. The Society owns George Washington's lap desk, Charles Willson Peale's portrait of Benjamin Franklin, and the iconic wampum belt that the Lenni Lenape tribe gave to Penn, symbolizing his honorable treatment of the local Native Americans.

When I first heard about the silver trophy bowl from a colleague who knew my penchant for buried treasure, I realized it was the perfect item through which to explore the dark secrets of Gowen, its original, and the Historical Society, its current owner. So I went to the Society's newly renovated library and spent a couple of days reading through ten Gowen speeches, three newspaper clippings, and a trove of papers.

Though virtually unknown today, in the 1870s Franklin B. Gowen was as powerful a robber baron as John D. Rockefeller, Andrew Carnegie, and Cornelius Vanderbilt. He was as cunning as Rupert Murdoch, as media savvy as Martha Stewart, and as ruthless as Enron's Ken Lay. The Gowen in the photograph owned by the Society looks surprisingly modern. You can easily imagine his square-jawed, stalwart face staring out from the front page of yesterday's *Wall Street Journal*.

Gowen's story begins in Philadelphia, where he was born in 1836 to a family of Episcopalian Irish immigrants. By age twenty-three, the ambitious young man had bought and lost his first coal mine. Within three years, his gift for oratory had secured him membership in the bar and election as district attorney for Schuylkill County, Pennsylvania. Gowen was later hired to head the legal department of the Philadelphia and Reading Railroad, and in 1870, at the age of thirty-four, he was elected company president.

Gowen's railroad monopolized the shipping of anthracite, which, because it burned clean and hot, was the fuel of choice for industry and homes. He ran his railroad like a dictator, its vast network carrying coal from the fields of northeastern Pennsylvania south to the ports of Philadelphia. But this ruthless railroad magnate wanted to monopolize more than shipping. He wanted to control the source of the wealth itself: the coal mines of Pennsylvania's lower anthracite region. Three hurdles stood in his way. First, he had to convince the Pennsylvania legislature to allow him to mine coal. Gowen quickly set up a subsidiary, the Philadelphia and Reading Coal and Iron Company, and through a political sleight of hand gained the right to mine coal and to borrow as much money as he needed.

The second hurdle was to persuade the owners of the smaller coal companies to sell out to him. Gowen doubled then doubled again the shipping rate for coal, driving many of the companies into bankruptcy. By the end of the 1870s, the Philadelphia and Reading Coal and Iron Company owned 125,000 acres of Pennsylvania's richest coal lands, the largest holdings in the world.

The third hurdle in Gowen's devious strategy was to end the labor strife that was slicing into coal industry profits. After decades of fighting against management's unfettered control over jobs, wages, housing, and even the price of food in the company store, the miners had finally organized the Workingmen's Benevolent Association. Miners spent their entire lives in these deep-pit dungeons, blasting coal from walls, digging it out, filling carts, and pulling them up to the surface. No wonder they needed a union to carry their cause.

Franklin Benjamin Gowen, determined to wipe out the Workingmen's Benevolent Association, accused it of harboring a seditious band of terrorists known as the Molly Maguires. In Ireland, the Molly Maguires were a secret society of Catholic patriots who fought to rid the nation of its hated English Protestant landlords. By 1870 Pennsylvania's coal towns were filled with Irish immigrants—including some Mollies, at least according to Gowen.

In 1875, Gowen secretly wrote to Allan Pinkerton of the Pinkerton National Detective Agency. Pinkerton hired a young Irishman to infiltrate the Workingmen's Benevolent Association. Two years later, when its members struck for fair wages, Gowen brought in Pinkerton's special police. The strike led to sabotage, then to the murder of ten mine bosses.

The shootings stunned the nation. America was already suffering the aftermath of a bloody Civil War and reeling from streams of immigrants who flooded the nation. Now they learned that Irish miners were tyrannizing and murdering in the once peaceful hills of Pennsylvania. A master of media manipulation, Gowen took advantage of the miners' crimes to tarnish the entire cause of organized labor through the purple-prose advertisements he placed in major newspapers.

In 1876, in a courtroom packed with sightseers and reporters, the accused miners were brought to trial for murder. All of the alleged defendants were Irish Catholics, but Protestants were selected for the jury. Franklin B. Gowen stepped in as lawyer for the prosecution, his commanding presence filling the courtroom. "For the first time, after struggling under a reign of terror that has extended over twenty years, we are placed front to front with the inner workings of a secret association," Gowen declaimed. The jury deliberated only one hour before returning the verdict of first-degree murder.

New arrests rapidly followed. By the end of 1877, ten miners had died at the end of the hangman's noose. Before it ended, forty-one people were convicted of felonies and twenty miners were put to death, including some who appeared innocent. Though labor strife continued, the Workingmen's Benevolent Association was crushed forever.

The case of the Mollie Maguires blazed across newspapers around the nation and the world. Detective Allan Pinkerton authored a sensationally popular novel, *The Molly Maguires and the Detective* (1877), which was later adapted into a stage play. Later, even Arthur Conan Doyle got into the act: his book *The Valley of Fear* (1914–1915) features an encounter between detective Sherlock Holmes and the dreaded Molly Maguires.

Franklin B. Gowen was hailed as a national hero. According to an April 1882 edition of the *Philadelphia Inquirer*, on the eve of his proposed trip to England to meet with his British investors, a delegation of mine owners appeared in Gowen's office and surprised him with "one of the handsomest silver and gold centre pieces ever manufactured in this country."

The oval bowl is big enough to bathe a toddler in. It stands more than fifteen inches high, eighteen inches wide, and thirty inches long. The base is festooned with laurel wreaths, the Greek symbol of victory, and features a massive silver specimen of anthracite surrounded by the picks, spades, and shovels of the miners' trade. The interior is swathed in gold; on the exterior are four medallions in gold mounting, two engraved with names of the eighteen coal barons who gave Gowen the bowl. One medallion portrays Josiah White, a founder of the anthracite coal industry, another Gowen. Around the top runs an inscription: "Presented to Franklin B. Gowen, as a Token of our Grateful Remembrance of his Services in Suppressing Lawless Violence and Re-Establishing Security for Life and Property in the Anthracite Coal Regions of Pennsylvania."

There is some poignancy in the fact that Gowen received his glorious trophy not at the peak of success but on the precipice of failure. Soon after he won this battle to save his company, he lost the war. Between 1871 and 1875, Gowen had borrowed $69 million—almost $1 billion in today's currency—to purchase coal fields and finance their development. He believed that America's burgeoning economy would spur an unlimited demand for anthracite. What he failed to foresee was a nationwide depression that dramatically cut coal consumption. In 1880 the Philadelphia and Reading went bankrupt. Gowen lost and then regained the presidency. Four years later, after a number of valiant attempts to borrow money and pay off creditors, Franklin Benjamin Gowen stepped down as president. A year later, he was found in a Washington, D.C., hotel room, shot to death by his own hand.

After Gowen's death, the bowl was passed through his family until 1963, when they donated it to the Historical Society of Pennsylvania. Over the years it was featured in an exhibit at the Houston Museum of Fine Arts, displayed a couple of times at the Society itself, and used to serve punch at its parties. However, Gowen's bowl may never appear there again. The bowl, along with most of the rest of the Society's treasured artifacts and art, has left its home forever.

Why would any historical society—especially one of the nation's oldest and most prominent—relinquish the icons that made its name? The reason lies in the second story that Gowen's bowl holds: the story of the Historical Society of Pennsylvania. In its own way, it's as dramatic as Gowen's. It's also emblematic of the struggles that many nineteenth-century institutions face when confronted with the exigencies of contemporary life.

This story begins in 1976, the year Philadelphia and the nation celebrated the bicentennial of the American Revolution. While the event failed to draw the millions of visitors its Philadelphia planners envisioned, it did spur local historical organizations to consider the public outside its doors. As the city's history leader, the Historical Society of Pennsylvania decided to enter this new world of public history and place its treasures on display. Fortuitously, funding organizations also shared this interest, most notably the National Endowment for the Humanities, at the time a relatively new federal government agency.

This public stance represented something new for the Society, which, like many of its ilk, had been founded as a research library serving scholars, genealogists, and of course, Philadelphia's founding families. By the 1970s, it had acquired vast documentary collections: 20 million manuscripts, 300,000 graphics, 7,500 maps, and 600,000 books, pamphlets, serials, and microfilm reels. More by happenstance than by design, it had also amassed approximately 11,000 pieces of art and artifacts, including Gowen's bowl. These, which the Society called the "museum collection," had never taken center stage.

In 1982 the Historical Society of Pennsylvania hired a curator for the museum collection and an able director of education, Cynthia Little, and launched a series of exhibits and programs. That's when I first got to know the place and its staff. As associate director of Philadelphia's 300th anniversary celebration, in 1983, I teamed with Cindy in the production of a traveling history exhibit that toured the city's neighborhoods in a retrofitted bus, funded by the National Endowment for the Humanities.

By the late 1980s the Society was ready to take another bold step. In December 1989 it opened the largest and most expensive exhibit in its history, *Finding Philadelphia's Past: Visions and Revisions.* The show was intended as a permanent installation that would wow the public and dispel the widely held impression of the Society as a preserve for the elite. The scholars and curators who crafted it sought to present a complex portrait of history's ambiguities. They incorporated just about every type of object and state-of-the-art exhibition technique: the icons of Pennsylvania history, the stuff of ordinary people, text, audio and video recordings, and even live actors portraying fictionalized characters from the past.

The scholars and curators were delighted with the show, and so was the Society's board, especially when the exhibit garnered many positive reviews in the local and national press. But, despite the quality of artifacts, quantity of exhibition technology, and the largest promotional effort ever, *Finding Philadelphia's Past* proved too complex for the general public. It also didn't help that the Society's stately but somewhat intimidating building was located near the central business district, far off the tourist trail. The exhibition drew only 7,000 visitors during 1990, its first full year of operation.

At the same time the show was being assembled, the Society was searching for a new leader. It selected Susan Stitt, who had served for fourteen years as director of the Museums at Stony Brook, a history and art museum on Long Island. Stitt had worked at the Historical Society of Pennsylvania in the 1960s so knew the place. Her national standing, stellar academic training and administrative credentials, and especially her fund-raising acumen impressed the board. She was the first woman and first professional president of the Historical Society of Pennsylvania.

Stitt, as it turned out, had much in common with Franklin Benjamin Gowen. Like the coal baron whose silver trophy sat in storage, Susan Stitt was arrogant, outspoken, and unstoppable.

Most people thought that the Historical Society of Pennsylvania was as well heeled as the families whose papers and heirlooms it housed. But looks can be deceiving. Behind its patrician façade, the Society was in terrible shape.

When Susan Stitt arrived in early 1990, she was shocked with what she found: a $200,000 deficit, a $250,000 overrun in the budget for *Finding Philadelphia's Past*, and a financial system that couldn't track the finances. The building was dated and disorganized; broken windows were covered with chicken wire. The documentary collections were in desperate need of care, many still in the boxes in which they had arrived decades earlier. A number of scholarly projects and patriotic, genealogical, and lineage societies were ensconced in offices. The staff was exhausted and disgruntled, working from desks set in collections storage rooms.

"My office was wedged into the storage area for eighteenth-century books," said Cindy Little, who later shared her experiences with me, along with her copy of Sally Griffith's *Serving History in a Changing World: The Historical Society of Pennsylvania in the Twentieth Century*, which the Society commissioned for its 175th anniversary. The book chronicles the sad saga that unfolded.

Susan Stitt took a long, hard look at the situation. She looked at the empty exhibit gallery, the cramped and disorganized building, the confused bookkeeping system, and the burgeoning deficit. She looked at the manuscript collections that had been seriously neglected while the Society focused on trying to attract the general public. She looked at the preferential treatment afforded to some researchers whom the staff serviced quickly while others waited. She looked at the organizations and scholarly programs that took up space and paid little or no rent. She came to the conclusion that the Society was serving too many constituencies and none of them well. Change, major change, was needed— and fast.

The first order of business was to gain control of the financial books. A financial management firm spent months trying to figure them out. They soon revealed a much darker situation. "Susan told me the place was hemorrhaging money at the rate of $50,000 a month," said Cindy Little, who became one of her closest advisors.

The second objective was to gain control of the staff. Some were let go to make budget; the rest were reorganized into a more functional structure. Cindy was promoted to vice president of interpretation and joined the management team.

The third objective was to gain control of the premises. Soon the special perks were eliminated and the scholarly projects, patriotic, genealogical, and lineage societies asked to leave. In record time, Stitt had alienated three of the Society's most important constituencies: scholars, staffers, and old-line Philadelphians.

At the same time, Stitt was formulating a strategy to tighten the mission of this august—but secretly struggling—institution. It was the nation's largest independent research center on Early American and Pennsylvania history. It owned one of the largest genealogical collections on the East Coast. This was where the Historical Society of Pennsylvania should focus. It should become a world-class research library.

Cindy frowned as she recalled Susan Stitt's strategy. "The idea to narrow the mission was nothing new: the minutes of the board meetings show they had discussed it for years. But the board never really realized its implications."

The decision to focus on the documentary collections raised another issue: what to do with the museum collection, the cream of Philadelphia's material culture. Susan Stitt had the answer. It had to go in order to make room for better staff offices and document collections storage and a reading room for researchers. The museum collection had to be de-accessioned.

De-accessioning, removing collections from collecting institutions, happens more often than most people realize. Museums, archives, and special collections libraries often de-accession items that were acquired in earlier days when directors were more acquisitive and the rules of collections care more forgiving. Sometimes directors were willing to accept piles of dross to secure the diamond. Other times, they acquired materials to satisfy a board member or wealthy donor in search of a tax deduction.

"People would stop by the Society on their way to their summer home in Maine, drop off something, and later forget about it," said Cindy Little.

Whatever the reasons, the fact is that much of what's buried in storage—not only at the Historical Society of Pennsylvania but also at most collecting institutions everywhere—has little or no connection with the organization that owns it. That's one of the main reasons there's so much stuff that no one sees.

Beginning in the late 1970s, a whole new generation of professionals emerged from the nation's new graduate programs in museums studies: managers, curators, archivists, educators, and conservators. They were guided by a new philosophy that combined sound business practice with a commitment to quality collections management. As these recent graduates moved into jobs at collecting institutions, they found much that didn't fit the mission. That's where de-accessioning came in.

There are a number of ways to de-accession. You can donate an item or trade it to another institution for something else that better fits your mission. You can sell it to another non-profit organization or to a private individual at auction. Museum professionals believe in de-accessioning because it eliminates the expense of caring for irrelevant materials. Boards like it because the proceeds from sales help fill the gaps in the budget, gaps that come, in part, from the higher salaries of professionally trained staff and improvements in collections care.

Susan Stitt faced a very tough problem: what to do with Gowen's bowl plus 11,000 more artifacts and artworks. Her solution was bold, actually revolutionary for a staid town like Philadelphia, and, as it turned out, the beginning of her downfall.

Stitt proposed to de-accession almost everything to an institution that didn't even exist. She decided what Philadelphia needed was a grand, new museum, a major history center filled with dazzling exhibits that would charm the locals and the hundreds of thousands of tourists who came to visit Independence Hall and the Liberty Bell. She knew of the successes of history centers recently built in Minnesota and other states. Philadelphia's, Stitt explained, would not only showcase the Society's treasures, but those from other local history museums in financial trouble.

Excited by this visionary concept, the board agreed to explore whether a new history center represented a viable option. If it didn't work out, if the money couldn't be found to build the history center, then other de-accessioning options would be explored. The board established a history center study group and, in 1995, began meeting with foundation executives, government and tourism officials, and board members of museums in financial trouble. Based on the positive response, a history center committee was set up with some outside representatives and began to look for money to build it.

I entered this picture in 1996, when I was hired as executive director of one of the financially challenged institutions slated for the history center: the Atwater Kent Museum. On my first day on the job, Susan Stitt invited me to lunch and spent most of it telling me that my job was not to run the museum, but rather to guide it to its demise so that its collections could go to the proposed history center. I related Stitt's astonishing pronouncement to the Atwater Kent's board chairman, Fred Lindquist, a recently retired executive with dead-on judgment. He said, "Don't worry about the history center. It will never happen. Just keep your nose down and focus on the museum."

Lindquist was right. While the history center excited the Society's board and some cultural leaders, it failed to excite prospective donors. When the effort was subsequently disbanded, the Society was left with the same problem: what to do with the museum collection.

Board and staff engaged in long and often heated debates as they carefully studied the options. What, if any, treasures should be kept in the permanent collection and what should go? Should any of the objects be sold? Could the proceeds be used to finance renovation of the building into a world-class research library? There were no clear answers because, at the time, the museum industry itself was debating the ethics of de-accessioning. Some believed that the proceeds from de-accessioned items should be restricted to the purchase of new ones. Others thought professional ethics allowed dollars to be directed toward any collections costs, including new security and environmental systems and building renovation. A team of research library experts was brought in; its report raised a host of other issues. It was all very confusing, very difficult to know the right thing to do.

By this time, the Historical Society of Pennsylvania was well down the road toward its goal. It had even hired Philadelphia's most renowned architecture firm to renovate the building into a research library. It now needed to make room for it by moving thousands of artifacts and paintings out of the building. It also needed millions of dollars to transform the first floor into an expansive library reading room and to install new storage furniture, windows, air conditioning, humidifiers, and security. While the Society had begun its own fund-raising campaign, the proceeds from the sale of some valuable art and artifacts would certainly help meet the goal.

In a city like Philadelphia, where there's so much history and history matters so much, this kind of story couldn't stay hidden for long. In June 1997, the Society's lawyers petitioned the Court of Common Pleas of Philadelphia County, Orphans' Court Division, which oversees not-for-profit organizations. It sought permission to transfer or sell five items: an important and valuable painting by renowned artist John Singleton Copley to the Philadelphia Museum of Art; three possessions of Thomas Jefferson then on loan to his home, Monticello; and a statue of famed actor Edwin Forrest, which was slated to go to Freedom Theatre, an African American theater company that owned Forrest's North Philadelphia home. The petition included a full description of the plans for the entire museum collection. Most would go to the history center and, barring that, its art and artifacts would eventually be de-accessioned in other, unspecified ways. A month later, the *Chronicle of Higher Education*, a national publication read widely by the educational and museum industries, published an article revealing that the Society was about to disperse most of its museum collection.

"City History Society Seeks to Sell Its Art," blazed the front-page headline in the *Philadelphia Inquirer* a couple of days later. The first sentence read, "Quietly, with no public notice, the Historical Society of Pennsylvania has asked court approval to sell, barter or give away virtually its entire collection of art and artifacts—including some of the rarest and most valued treasures held by any institution in the country." It quoted Susan Stitt: "There is regret that this is an institution that never had an adequate capacity to care for everything. It still doesn't. We can't do everything." It also quoted a number of people who opposed the strategy, including a local historian who characterized the deaccessioning as "an evisceration" and "a betrayal of the public trust."

As it turned out, not everyone was enamored with the plan. Four members had resigned from the board; some of them, and a number of scholars and former staffers, were more than willing to take the issue public. They met secretly and hired a publicist.

Letters and phone calls flooded Society offices and board members' homes. Founding families were horrified that their precious heirlooms were about to go out the door—and perhaps even out of Philadelphia. Chief Roy Crazy Horse of the Lenni Lenape tribe called, worried that the Society was going to sell the iconic wampum belt. Scholars expressed concern that the Society's intellectual integrity was about to be destroyed. Foundation executives and government officials raised serious questions. When funders raise serious questions, there's trouble ahead.

"We received hysterical phone calls, vicious hate mail, and even a death threat," remembered Cindy Little. "You'd never know who was on the line when you picked up the phone, what crazy would start yelling."

Board and staff were stunned. Faced with a large and growing deficit and a building in disrepair, they believed they had made a strategic and prudent decision to hone the mission and shed what didn't comply with it. They thought they were doing the right thing, the best thing under the circumstances, for the institution and the collections. But somehow, things were getting out of hand. "The other voices were so loud and over the top we couldn't get heard," remembered Cindy.

The Society hired its own public relations expert and began fighting back. The official response appeared in the August 6, 1997, edition of the *Philadelphia Inquirer*. In it, Susan Stitt and the board chair carefully explained the thinking behind the decision to focus on the documentary materials for scholarly research. They emphasized that the Society was making every effort to keep the collections "in the public domain and in Philadelphia with local museums and nonprofit institutions."

The effort was too little, too late. The following Sunday the *Philadelphia Inquirer* published an editorial that acknowledged that the Society had been discussing its change of mission for several years but warned that "fears to move civic treasures into private control can't be dismissed with a patrician wave of the hand." This was, after all, "the city's patrimony."

A city's patrimony is a precious thing. And here at the most distinguished historical society in one of the nation's most historically conscious cities, the issue of stewardship came to the fore. The Society's art and artifacts carried, in the minds of the public, the resonance of relics. While the Society was their steward, they belonged to the public. These were Philadelphia's icons; their disposition was a matter of highest concern.

When Cindy revisited these turbulent times, she got angry all over again. "The whole experience was very painful," she said. "But it's a mistake to focus on Susan Stitt, because you miss the underlying structural problems. The Society was filled with structural problems: the structure itself was in terrible shape. When Susan was hired, there was no board-approved personnel manual, no system for preparing job descriptions, placing ads, or annually evaluating staff performance. Since the issue of security had never received adequate attention, those connected with the organizations whose offices were in the building could wander through the collections at will. The place was run like a private club. It needed to run like a professional organization."

The Historical Society of Pennsylvania was not unique. Around the same time, the New York Historical Society was struggling for survival because of many of the same financial and structural problems. In fact, the New York institution had tried to de-accession many of its holdings but backed off because of public protests.

"I understand why people connected to the organization were angry," I said. "But why do you think the public response was so virulent?"

Cindy thought for a minute. "People didn't want to pay to keep the treasures at the Historical Society, they didn't want to visit them on display. But they somehow needed to know that the treasures were still there. There's a deep-seated, emotional chord, a sentimental civic attachment to these items."

The Society was trapped. It would not reverse its decision to become a world-class library. Because of the public outcry, it could not break up the collections by de-accessioning individual items or transfer the entire lot to an institution outside the city's borders. The only course of action was to find a single, local museum that would properly care for all of them and place them on public display.

There was only one choice: the Atwater Kent Museum, a place relatively small and definitely poor. As its executive director, responsible for balancing the budget, I couldn't quite see the advantage of assuming responsibility for the Society's museum collection. True, the art and artifacts would dramatically upgrade the museum's standing. But along with the few gems came piles of stuff, along with the burden of caring for them. Our cramped storage crypt couldn't hold them, and even if it could, it lacked the stable environmental conditions that such materials demand. The costs would bloat the already overtaxed budget. The Atwater Kent didn't need to acquire the Society's treasures. If we ever decided to feature them in an exhibit, we could always borrow them.

I was in the minority. The Atwater Kent's board was eager for the Society's jewels to complement its eclectic collection. A transfer agreement that includes many strings and multiple conditions was signed by the Society and the museum in July 1999.

Meanwhile, renovation of the Historical Society was moving forward. Its building was closed to researchers beginning in late 1997. A month later the FBI announced the arrests of two insiders: a twenty-year employee and an electrician who had done work there. Over ten years, they had stolen some 200 items. At a news conference, Susan Stitt attributed the thefts to "under-capitalization and under-funding of this society for 170 years." She carefully explained that the Society had conducted its first inventory in the 1980s and even then some items were discovered missing. When the building closed for renovation, staff members were able to conduct the first complete inventory. That's when the theft was revealed.

"Susan didn't have to go public," Cindy Little pointed out. "Many museums hide this kind of theft because they know it undermines the public's confidence. She knew it was the right thing and she never hesitated."

But the theft again raised the specter of the Society's failure of stewardship. In July 1998, Susan Stitt resigned her post as president of the Historical Society of Pennsylvania. Cindy Little and a colleague were asked to step in as co-presidents. "We decided we had to finish the work we had begun. We owed it to the institution."

I had resigned as executive director of the Atwater Kent Museum by the time Franklin B. Gowen's bowl moved from the Society's storage crypts to crypts in rented space. Because the museum didn't have the money, the Society ended up paying for moving, storage, and curatorial staff.

Franklin Benjamin Gowen, railroad president, and Susan Stitt, museum president, shared a penchant for power. Gowen ended labor strife, but at the cost of ten miners' lives. He built the Philadelphia and Reading Railroad into one of the world's largest corporations, and watched it crash into bankruptcy. He succeeded beyond the wildest expectations of anyone but himself and failed on the grandest of scales. Gowen loved power better than life itself and when he lost it, his life was not worth living.

Like Gowen, Susan Stitt's life was filled with great achievement and tragedy. Through the best of intentions and unstoppable determination, she succeeded in her contentious quest to narrow the focus, and thus preserve the future, of one of our nation's most distinguished historical institutions. Her great tragedy is that she failed to realize the psychic power of the civic icons under her stewardship. Her life, like Gowen's, ended under a cloud, her reputation tainted by her tenure at the Society. Tragically, she died of cancer three years after resigning as president.

But, when you think about it, there's a bitter irony here. When Franklin Gowen did the wrong thing, when he spurred the death of twenty people, he was rewarded with a majestic silver trophy bowl. When Susan Stitt did the right thing, when she followed her heart and her high professional standards, she was forced to resign.

"These old institutions are very tough to change," said Cindy Little. People don't like to hear bad news and Susan delivered a lot of it."

Today Cynthia Little has joined the Historical Society of Pennsylvania's art and artifacts at the Atwater Kent Museum, though the collection is kept in a rented storage space. She recently featured Gowen's bowl in an exhibit on hidden museum treasures.

"I think the Society's collections actually fit well at the Atwater Kent," Cindy said. "And the Historical Society of Pennsylvania is a much better, much stronger institution, a place where researchers can do their work and the documentary collections are safe. It all kind of worked out in the end."

PESSARIES

Pessaries
Courtesy of the Mütter Museum, College of Physicians of Philadelphia

PESSARIES

Mütter Museum of the College of Physicians
of Philadelphia

When I asked Gretchen Worden, director of Philadelphia's strangest museum, to show me something the public never gets to see, she didn't hesitate. "Pessaries," she said, with a wicked grin. "Pessaries."

Pessaries? I'd never heard of them.

"The Mütter Museum owns 267 pessaries, which makes it one of the most comprehensive collections anywhere," said Worden proudly.

Museums are more than the stuff they store and the exhibits they stage. They're also about the people who work in them. The most distinctive type is the curator, the ruler of the collection. Gretchen Worden was the quintessential curator, proof positive that the best museums match their style with their staff. She was inquisitive, acquisitive, and a consummate raconteur. She loved plaster casts of conjoined twins, dried placentas revealing obstetric anomalies, and President Grover Cleveland's tumor. She was mad for obsolete medical instruments, obscure medical terminology, and antiquated museum cabinetry. This was the kind of stuff featured in the Mütter Museum of the College of Physicians of Philadelphia, where Worden served as director. I'd gone to visit her because she was so very colorful and the place so very strange.

Worden, the daughter of an oil company geologist, was born in Shanghai, China, in 1947. Her entire professional life was spent at the Mütter Museum, beginning as an assistant curator in 1975 and working her way up to director eleven years later. More stylish than the typical curator, whose attire generally runs toward the dowdy, Worden sported a chic shag of brown hair, vivid blue eye shadow, and a lean, black wardrobe. She never married; her work was her life, and though the pay was low, she believed her job was the best in the world.

"If I won the lottery, I would endow the Mütter," she told me.

"Let's go take a look at the pessaries," she said, leading me from the elegant marble lobby of the College of Physicians, down a flight of stairs to the basement, and into a well-ordered storage room lined with metal cabinets. The pessaries were stored in the "ob-gyn" section among drawers labeled "obstetrical forceps," "pelvi-meters," and "hysterectomy/ ovariotomy instruments." Worden pulled out one of the four drawers labeled "pessaries" and slid back the wooden cover. Inside, carefully arranged in dozens of small cubicles, were the devices, each tagged or labeled with a tiny accession number corresponding to the drawer's inventory list. As she opened one drawer after another, I found myself on a surreal walk through time and women's pelvises.

As Worden explained it, pessaries were the treatment of choice for genital prolapse, the oldest recorded gynecological condition. When the muscles and ligaments that support women's pelvic organs become stretched or damaged, the uterus or vagina can prolapse, or drop, against the wall of the vagina. Sometimes the organ drops down so far that the bulge sticks out through the vaginal opening. Most often this happens from poorly conducted or numerous childbirths or peculiar sexual practices. As women get older, the condition can worsen.

For 4,000 years, physicians who sought to address this condition inserted a pessary to keep things in place. Sometimes, though not frequently, they do so today.

"How did physicians get the pessary up there?" I asked.

"How do you get anything up there?" responded Gretchen Worden, grinning. "You lie back and shove it up."

An astonishing variety of objects have been shoved up women. The Mütter Museum's pessaries are made of gold, silver, and iron; hard and soft rubber; Vulcanite, Bakelite, and glass. One was a metal hoop about five inches long with a mean-looking, two-inch-long, metal finger at the end. There was something resembling a coat button, which sat atop something resembling a bent bobby pin. There was a one-inch-wide metal ring with three springs attached to it, each spring with an oval metal button stuck on the end. The Gehrung anteversion pessary was a two-inch-long horseshoe made of hard rubber. The Thomas-Cutter stem pessary was an eight-inch-long pipe with a ring about two inches down the stem.

Pessary number 17520.22 carried the description "Old silver ball pessary worn for many years by a woman, only removed when its corrosion and sharp edges induced inflammation." I peered down at a palm-size sphere of cracked and tarnished sheet metal. It looked like a sick joke for a Christmas-tree ornament.

"Why are there so many different types?" I asked in awe.

"Uteruses come in a variety of shapes, and so do pessaries," explained Worden. "One shape doesn't fit all, until you get to the more flexible materials of the twentieth century. Most were invented by gynecologists who represent a particularly inventive medical specialty."

A hundred years ago, museums like the Mütter were an essential element of high-quality medical institutions. Filled with human bones, wax models, and fetuses floating in alcohol and formaldehyde, they were assembled to help students and physicians develop an eye for the normal and the diseased. As technological advancements made medical museums obsolete, it was left to places off the beaten track like the College of Physicians of Philadelphia to preserve the tradition.

"Museums of anatomy and pathology were especially important in places like Philadelphia that banned the anatomical study of the recently deceased until the late nineteenth century," Worden explained. "Many cities banned such studies."

The Mütter has been collecting medical instruments since 1871, which is where its pessaries fit in. They are a small part of a large cache of obsolete Catlin knives, obstetrical forceps, sutures, ophthalmoscopes, bronchoscopes, volume ventilators, and other items—some one of a kind, others mass produced—that once filled physician offices and hospital rooms. The Mütter owns Florence Nightingale's sewing kit, Pierre Curie's quartz-piezo electrometer, and a full-scale model of the Emerson iron lung, invented in Philadelphia.

In sharp contrast to the tidy storage room, every surface of Worden's office was covered with something. Five vases filled with dead flowers sat on the sill of a streaked window. Atop the filing cabinets were conjoined felt dragons and china puppies; an eighteen-inch model of a human skeleton with a wooden parakeet on its shoulder; a toy Wild Rockin' Rat that sang and danced to "Wild Thing" when its foot was pressed; and a display box with twenty-eight skulls the size of pinky fingernails labeled "Worden Skull Collection." Piles of papers covered her desk; more were stacked on the floor nearby. A copy of the *Paranoid Times* with the headline "The World Could End Tomorrow and You May Die" hung near a photocopied page from the spring 1994 edition of *Walt Whitman Quarterly* featuring seven photos of a naked old man captioned "Thomas Eakins' Multiple Photographs of Whitman Naked?"

The clutter was deceptive. Gretchen Worden knew exactly where everything was. She dove into a drawer, found the pessary file, and pulled out chapters from medical textbooks, excerpts from encyclopedias, brochures from pessary manufacturers, and even a couple of articles she authored.

I learned that the Mütter Museum's plethora of pessaries was part of a very long tradition. Early Egyptian papyrus from 2000 BCE described the condition of prolapse; Cleopatra herself noted this female ailment and was prescribed an astringent solution for application on her secret flower. Hippocrates, the great Greek physician, followed a more assertive approach. He tied his women patients upside down to a ladder-like frame, shook the frame rapidly up and down, and let the forces of gravity drive the organ up to its proper place.

By 350 BCE, physicians were inserting objects in women's private parts to block descending organs. Diocles of Carystol is credited with the invention of the pomegranate and vinegar pessary. He cut a pomegranate in half, dipped it into vinegar, and shoved it up. Other early physicians enticed the bulge inside by decorating women's heads and necks with "pleasant fumigations" while at the same time placing nasty-smelling things next to their deltas of Venus.

The saga of the pessary continued through the Middle Ages, which was not a particularly innovative era in gynecological medicine. With the dawning of the Renaissance, physicians were inserting pessaries made of bound sponges dipped in wax and covered with oil or butter and pessaries made of gold, brass, and silver, kept in place by belts worn around the waist. In 1603, R. de Castro took a red-hot piece of iron, placed it near a woman's lotus flower, and frightened the bulge right back up.

The nineteenth century was the heyday of the pessary, and Philadelphia, America's leading medical center, became the pessary capital of the nation. The "Father of American Surgery," Philip Syng Physick, invented his famous globe pessary when he happened upon an old billiard ball and realized that it was just the thing to stabilize the uterus. Another Philadelphian, Dr. Hugh Lenox Hodge, modeled his famed Hodge pessary on the steel hook at the ends of fire shovels and tongs.

During the 1800s, the ins and outs of pessary placement fueled gynecological practices. In 1860, speaking for a large segment of his profession, Dr. Hodge stated that a properly designed pessary was a "sine qua non" in the relief of a panoply of symptoms, including weight, pain, spasms, cramps, nervous headaches, nervous stomachs, and depression. One observer from the period commented, "Fortunes were to be made by two groups of gynecologists—those who inserted pessaries and those who removed them." Not every physician was enamored with the devise. In 1866, the president of the New Hampshire Medical Society stated: "Pessaries, I suppose, are sometimes useful, but there are more than there is any necessity for. I do think that this filling the vagina with such traps, making a Chinese toy-shop of it, is outrageous."

Outrageous was an understatement. Why would any woman submit to this torture, let alone millions of women for thousands of years? I started thinking about how many women and infants died during childbirth, before the advent of antiseptics. Pessaries were a less-than-subtle form of contraception, these glass balls and metal stirrups keeping the men folk at bay. In fact, the modern cervical cap, used as a contraceptive devise, is a type of pessary.

Happily, by the late 1800s, the medical debate over use of the pessary had more or less ended as surgical repair of genital organ prolapses became more common. Women were also treated with cold-water hip-baths, uterine "gymnastics," and the application of leeches. Eventually, most pessaries were consigned to dusty drawers and trash heaps. Today their use is more limited. The Milex Silicone pessary, donated to the Mütter by a sympathetic gynecologist, is used only as a stopgap prior to surgery or on a long-term basis when surgery is too risky. Women are cautioned to remove and clean these pessaries frequently to prevent ulcers and nasty odors.

Like all curators, Worden's work was governed by stringent policies detailing what objects can be acquired; the environmental, storage and security requirements; and the conditions under which items can be de-accessioned. It's the curatorial staff that marks each one with a set of tiny numbers when it is accessioned, and then adds the information into the voluminous inventories that enable collecting institutions to know what they have and where it's kept. When a museum, like the Mütter, owns some 20,000 objects, knowing where each one is located becomes important, especially when a researcher or scholar stops by to see them.

The College of Physicians of Philadelphia is not a teaching institution but a private medical society. It was founded in 1787 to collect scientific and medical knowledge, to promote its use for the public welfare, and to encourage the highest professional standards among its members. The College is Philadelphia's medical history in a nutshell, and no city's is richer. Philadelphia was home to America's first hospital, Pennsylvania Hospital, founded in 1751, and to the Medical College of Pennsylvania, the first medical school for women. An array of medical giants conducted their seminal work here; their possessions can still be found, scattered throughout the city. The elegant home of Philip Syng Physick of pessary fame is a historic house museum in the Society Hill neighborhood, open to the public. Documents owned by Benjamin Rush, the "Father of American Psychiatry" and signer of the Declaration of Independence, are at the Library Company of Philadelphia. The archives of the "Father of American Neurology," S. Weir Mitchell, are stored in the College of Physicians' vast library, along with about a million other manuscripts. Hundreds of medical instruments, anatomical models, and pieces of human remains are on display in the Mütter Museum.

From Worden's office, it was a quick walk through a doorway into this cabinet of medical wonders. The origins of the Mütter Museum date back to 1858 when Thomas Dent Mütter, professor of surgery at Jefferson Medical College, donated 1,700 items to the College of Physicians of Philadelphia. Mütter also donated an endowment of $30,000, the proceeds to be used to care for and expand the collection and to pay for a curator and a lecturer. Mütter insisted that the College of Physicians construct a fireproof building to house his collection within five years of his donation, so the College built one and, in 1863, moved the items in.

Soon the public stopped by for a look-see. In the 1860s, a visitor to Philadelphia with a medical appetite and a little time on his or her hands could visit pathological museums at Pennsylvania Hospital, Philadelphia General Hospital, the Pennsylvania College, the Homeopathic Medical College, and the Female Medical College. This tourist could also select from among the popular anatomic museums, but the European Museum, established in 1858, was open to "gentlemen only."

In 1910 the College of Physicians of Philadelphia moved into its current home, an impressive brick building designed by Cope and Stewardson, and the Mütter Museum was installed inside. Today's visitors can view many of Dr. Mütter's most memorable possessions, displayed much the way they were when the museum opened. These include a wax model of a Parisian widow with a six-inch horn extending from her forehead, and the skeleton of a woman whose rib cage was squeezed like a lemon from tying her corset too tight. The original glass-fronted oak cabinets circle the walls, their shelves lined with objects that are labeled with detailed medical terminology. Specimens are arranged according to the affected organ system. Many float in liquid-filled bottles: a mammary tumor in formaldehyde; bits and pieces of urinary calcia extracted over fifty-five years by urinary surgeon Dr. G. N. J. Sommers of Trenton, New Jersey; a Buddha-like fetus with anencephaly. "Anencephaly is characterized by a lack of brain," read the label.

"People love conjoined twins," said Worden, as she pointed out the plaster cast of the torsos of the famed Siamese twins Chang and Eng, who were autopsied in the College of Physicians. The cast sits atop a case housing the twins' actual connected livers, which were removed before their remains were sent home to North Carolina for burial by their wives and their twenty-one children. Nearby was a glass-topped cabinet featuring an exhibit entitled "Siamese Twins in Fact and Fiction." On display were two-headed troll dolls, Siamese twins cartoons, Siamese twins bendy toys, and a set of Freaks II trading cards with pictures of Siamese twins.

In a glass-top sarcophagus lay the blackened body of a woman who died in Philadelphia of yellow fever and whose body fat eventually decomposed into soap. I looked down at the sag of her ancient breasts; her toothless mouth gaped in a silent scream. A waist-high cabinet of drawers held the 2,000 safety pins, jacks, bits of food, and other items removed from the noses, mouths, and throats of the patients of physician Chevalier Jackson and his colleagues.

Down the flight of red-carpeted stairs, three skeletons hung like Day of the Dead puppets in a high case. One was the skeleton of a seven-and-a-half-foot giant, one was the skeleton of an average-size man, and one was the skeleton of Mary Ashberry, a three-and-a-half-foot dwarf who died in 1856 from childbirth.

While the Mütter's antiquated approach to museum display may appear confusing, it made perfect sense to Gretchen Worden. She believed that the role of the curator is to bring the objects forward and let them speak for themselves.

"Life is complicated," she explained. "You lie if you try to simplify things. As a curator, my role is to present the evidence and let others draw their own conclusions." Take, for example, the wall filled with 139 skulls from central and eastern Europe that look down on visitors.

"Why do all 139 need to be displayed?" I asked. "They all look the same to me."

"You have to look closely, train your eye, said Worden. "Each one is unique. That's what medical education is all about. If we just picked out one type of skull, then people would think that central and eastern Europeans all looked alike. The diversity is the message, and you can't illustrate it by eliminating diversity."

"I understand why it's important to preserve these medical specimens and models," I said looking around. "But why save the medical equipment? Why save the pessaries? After all, no one uses them anymore; they're obsolete."

"That's the very reason they need to be saved," responded Worden. "Take the Emerson iron lung from 1949," she said. "Sure it's obsolete, because there are vaccines, but in the 1950s this machine saved lives. You can see pictures or read about iron lungs or even pessaries, but you can't really understand how these devices were used or how they changed over time unless you experience them firsthand."

In her article "Steel Knives and Iron Lungs: Medical Instruments as Medical History," published by the College of Physicians, Worden brought this argument home. She wrote: "There are wonderful opportunities for historical research in collections of medical artifacts. The challenge is getting that message across to people who have read or written about medical history without considering the artifacts and mistakenly think that they are getting the whole story. The medical artifacts themselves can often speak as powerfully as written explanations."

That's really the point.

It's this rigorous adherence to tradition that makes the Mütter so memorable. And more are discovering it. The Mütter was profiled by the Discovery Channel, covered by the BBC, and featured on *NBC News* and *Dateline*. Gretchen Worden's quick wit and encyclopedic mind made her a welcomed guest on *The Late Show with David Letterman* when she brought along some very strange stuff to show television viewers. She invited some of the nation's most accomplished photographers to take pictures of their favorite objects and then featured their evocative and sometimes disquieting images in calendars that became holiday gift favorites. These efforts and Worden's unbounded enthusiasm boosted attendance at the Mütter from 5,000 to 65,000 during her tenure as director.

"Our biggest problem is that we're getting too many people," sighed Worden, expressing a view seldom heard from a museum director. The day I visited, about one hundred senior citizens, young couples on dates, and parents with children crowded in front of the cases.

Gretchen Worden died in August 2004 at age fifty-seven. She had suffered from cancer in childhood, and although it lay dormant for decades, it eventually took her life. I was among the collection of 800 family members and friends—society matrons, physicians, sideshow performers, museum professionals—who attended the memorial service. We sang hymns, watched clips of Worden on *Letterman*, and wept a bit. Following her explicit instructions, at the end of the tribute, we donned deelie-boppers—headbands topped with bouncing balls affixed to springs—and filed out to the tune of "Puttin' on the Ritz," one of her favorite songs.

Since Gretchen Worden never fulfilled her lifelong dream of endowing the Mütter Museum, her friends did it for her. Soon after her death, the College of Physicians began receiving donations in her name, which eventually led to the decision to raise more money and turn a storage room into a new gallery dedicated to her. Worden's portrait is now a permanent installation in the place she loved most, surrounded by approximately 300 items drawn from the collection, some of which have never been displayed before.

Gretchen would be pleased. But what will happen now that she's gone? Will her successors replace the out-of-date cabinetry and obscure labels? Will they remove the fetuses in bottles because they are not politically correct? Will they destroy the unique and authentic experience of this historic museum of pathology and anatomy, substituting the ersatz experience that's so ubiquitous in museums today? While the Mütter Museum seems as timeless as a tomb, it's actually as delicate as a feather. It could easily be blown away in the winds of modernity.

Every Valentine's Day, Gretchen liked to bring out the pessaries as a special treat for members of the Obstetrical Society of Philadelphia. Other than this annual appearance, during her tenure they lay buried in storage in the basement of the College of Physicians of Philadelphia, which seemed somehow fitting for devices that once lay buried inside women.

"Talk about your hidden treasures," she said to me once. "Only you and your gynecologist know for sure."

SKULL OF A PREHISTORIC PERUVIAN CHILD

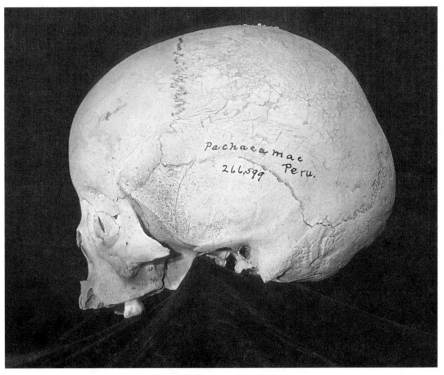

Skull of a Peruvian Child
Courtesy of the Smithsonian Institution, National Museum of Natural History

SKULL OF A PREHISTORIC PERUVIAN CHILD

Smithsonian Institution, National Museum of Natural History

A Peruvian child lay on his back, writhing in pain. During the last six months his distraught parents watched helplessly as their child became increasingly ill; they smelled his foul breath and saw his bleeding gums and the red, swollen lumps under the skin that burned like fire when touched. They knew babies and young children who suffered like this, but never a child as old as eleven, and most died. The child called out for food, he was hungry, but every bite was agony.

Within a few days the child was dead. His grieving parents carried his body a day's journey from their coastal town to the desert beyond. They carefully dressed the corpse, gently folded it into a fetal position, and buried it in an isolated graveyard, surrounded with pots of food that accompanied his spirit on its final journey.

Five or more centuries later, in 1920, *huaqueros*—hole diggers—in search of burial goods to sell on the antiquities market dug below the dry ground and uncovered the grave of the prehistoric child. In their rush for treasures, they tossed the skeleton up out of the grave and reached for the precious pottery and jewelry nearby. Later, an American scientist of Czech descent found the skull and placed it in a sack along with others he was recovering from the desert floor. The scientist, whose name was Aleš Hrdlička, transported the skull back to the place where he served as curator. Once there, he accessioned it with the catalog number 266599 and wrote the number and location of the find, Pachacamac, Peru, on the skull's crown. Then, he placed it in a storage drawer on the fourth floor of the Smithsonian Institution's National Museum of Natural History.

I've never been to prehistoric Peru and neither has Donald Ortner, a world-famous curator at the Smithsonian Institution's National Museum of Natural History, because the prehistoric era ended in the New World when Columbus arrived around 1492. But Ortner, who showed me the skull of the eleven-year-old, knows this story is true. He was able to look at it and diagnose scurvy, the terrible disease the child had when he died, from the skeletal abnormalities that remained.

Donald Ortner is a paleopathologist: an authority on disease in prehistoric humans. The field is very small—there are only about 1,400 practicing paleopathologists worldwide, and Ortner is one of three or four who practice full-time—and embraces a range of specialists, including archeologists and a fair number of practicing physicians. What's particularly intriguing to someone interested in museum collections is that without the hundreds of thousands of human skeletons stored in museums throughout the world, the field of paleopathology would not exist; there would be no paleopathologists to figure out what diseases these people had when they died. Paleopathologists create current science from old bones; their work is proof positive of the critical importance of museum holdings.

"Come down to the Smithsonian and I'll make you one of the world's leading experts in scurvy in prehistoric man," wrote Ortner in his email. Who could refuse such a tempting invitation? A couple of days later I was escorted by a volunteer to his office door.

I was lucky there was a guide. If you attempt to locate Donald Ortner's office without one, you may be lost forever in the National Museum of Natural History's endless labyrinth of corridors, offices, laboratories, and storage vaults; you might even eventually become one of the skeletons stored in the tall banks of drawers outside his third-floor office. Inside the drawers are thousands of human remains collected for the Smithsonian Institution over more than a century. One drawer Donald Ortner pulled out at my request held modern skeletons from St. Louis, Missouri. They had been dissected by medical students learning anatomy, then macerated to remove all their soft tissues. "Because of medical records, we know much about them, so they provide an important baseline for our research on archeological human burials," said Ortner. "They're beautiful specimens."

With a scanning electron microscope, x-rays, computer temography, a small magnifying loop, and his naked eye, Donald Ortner has used these and other human remains to diagnose tuberculosis, rheumatoid arthritis, rickets, leprosy, anemia, syphilis, and murder by gunshot and scalping. All of these conditions can leave traces on the bone.

One would think this line of work would lead to a pessimistic outlook on life. Donald Ortner has a wry sense of humor and an infectious enthusiasm for his work. While his desktop carries a sign that says "Faults I may have; being wrong isn't one of them," he is humble in the way of the most accomplished scientists: those who know the search for knowledge is never over.

"I'm not developing a cure for cancer, and sometimes I wonder if I've spent the last forty-five years fiddling while Rome burned. So why is this work important?" Ortner asked rhetorically. "Why is history important if we keep repeating past mistakes? Why do some non-Western societies without written history carefully transmit their past through the stories they tell their children? I believe that a desire to know about one's past is hard-wired in human beings."

"So, what can we know about this skull?" I asked the day I visited, pointing to the one with the number 266599 written in indelible ink on its crown. It was sitting on a trolley along with a couple of other skulls and bones in Ortner's office.

"This is the skull of a child who lived in Peru sometime between AD 900 and 1450. There's much we can't know. For example we can't tell whether it was male or female, but there's lots we can. You see these areas covered with many tiny pits," he said, pointing to the tops of both eye sockets and the sides in front of where the ears used to be, "well, that's evidence of scurvy. It remains a serious problem in many countries today where so many children are malnourished. It's caused by a lack of vitamin C, which is very important in making and maintaining healthy bones, blood vessels, and other connective tissue."

As Ortner began to unravel the skull's mysteries, I found myself in a private tutorial taught by one of the world's preeminent paleopathologists. We began with the disease itself.

Scurvy is caused by a deficiency of vitamin C, ascorbic acid. Found in citrus fruit, green vegetables, and other foods, Ortner explained, vitamin C is crucial in the formation of collagen, a protein in blood vessels and connective tissue: bones, tendons, and muscles. When people do not get enough vitamin C, they are less able to respond effectively to infectious diseases, like influenza, meningitis, pneumonia, and tuberculosis. Some primates are able to synthesize vitamin C, but not humans; we need a constant supply of vitamin C to stay healthy.

When people fail to ingest sufficient quantities of vitamin C, their collagen becomes defective. Blood vessels are easily ruptured by minor trauma, and bleeding occurs into the surrounding tissues. Even a trauma as minor as chewing can cause a hemorrhage, a dark swollen lump filled with blood under the skin. Blood outside the vessel wall is destructive; the immune system mobilizes to eliminate it.

"Let's take a look," Ortner said, picking up the Peruvian child's skull, which was missing its jawbone, or mandible. "This bone is the greater wing of the sphenoid. You can see it forms part of the lateral wall of the eye sockets," he said, turning the skull so I could look inside. "If you look closely, you can see the signs of scurvy on the external surface of both sides of the greater wing. This area should be dense and smooth, but it's porous. See the many tiny pits that penetrate through the bone? If the pits penetrate on only one side of the wing, it could be a sign of infection; when it's on both sides, it's almost a sure sign of scurvy. On skulls, the skeletal abnormalities of scurvy are almost always bilateral."

"Why does scurvy show there?" I asked.

"It's all about trauma," he explained. "Remember, the young Peruvian was so sick that even chewing caused damage. One of the major muscles for chewing passes over the greater wing of the sphenoid and connects with the mandible. Blood vessels occur between the sphenoid and the muscle. When our young Peruvian chewed, the muscle action over the greater wing of the sphenoid damaged the blood vessel, creating bleeding and a hemorrhage. This stimulated a vascular response in which additional blood vessels penetrated the sphenoid to provide the pathway for the body's clean-up mechanisms to attempt removal of the hemorrhage. Unfortunately the new blood vessels were also defective and vulnerable to the effects of muscle action and additional bleeding."

I placed my hands on either side of my eye sockets next to my ears and practiced chewing. As the muscles contracted, I felt my jawbone move toward and away from my greater wing of the sphenoid.

"Want to hold it?" offered Ortner, handing the skull to me, and all of a sudden I was holding the remains of a human being at least 500 years old.

"Why don't I need to wear curator's gloves?" I asked.

"The Peruvian child's been dead so long that there's no way it could contain pathogens that could hurt you," he replied. "And you can't hurt it because it's been handled so much that if we want to do a DNA test, we will have to take this into account."

I turned the skull slowly in my hands, studying it closely. It was six and three-quarters inches long with a crown crusted from sitting on the dry desert floor. The tops of both of the eye sockets and the greater wing of the sphenoid were covered with minuscule perforations, as if drilled by needles the size of cat whiskers.

"How do you know the child was eleven years old?" I asked.

"From the teeth; these are the six-year molars," he explained as he pointed to the child's two remaining teeth, one on each side of the top jaw near the rear. "They're a bit worn down. Next to them are the cavities for the twelve-year molars. You can see these molars were almost fully erupted from the root sockets," he said, sticking the point of his pen into one of the cavities. All that remained were three tiny root holes, surrounded by webs of tiny calcified filaments.

"Most often you see scurvy in infants and younger children, because their bones are still developing and they're most susceptible to malnutrition," Ortner continued. "This eleven-year-old is particularly old to show skeletal evidence of the disease. But though scurvy weakened him, he likely died from something else. Those with scurvy are very vulnerable to other disorders, particularly infection."

Called the "stinking disease" because of the foul breath of its sufferers, scurvy is an ancient plague that devastated civilizations throughout many parts of the world. It is not the kind of disease like polio that someone diagnosed, discovered a cure for, and the problem was solved. Instead, people living in different time periods in different parts of the world discovered different ways to treat its symptoms long before they knew its cause. Some North American tribes knew about scurvy and trained the European settlers to drink herbal teas, or to eat pemmican, a mix of dried meat and fruit, rich in vitamin C.

Scurvy was particularly virulent among soldiers and sailors whose military rations seldom contained adequate amounts of vitamin C. It wasn't until the 1700s that Europeans began to understand the miraculous benefits of citrus. British naval commander James Lind was the first to encourage the British navy to make citrus fruit available to sailors; that's why British sailors are called "limeys," after the limes they sucked during long sea voyages.

Sadly, the prehistoric parents of Ortner's Peruvian child did not know how to slow his rapid decline: the potatoes that were likely the centerpiece of his diet are poor in vitamin C. The tragedy is that with proper nutrition, the child could have been completely cured. When children with scurvy are given fresh vitamin C, they show signs of recovery within twenty-four hours, and are eventually cured. That's because as children grow into teenagers, their bones actually regenerate.

With so many skeletal remains to choose from—the National Museum of Natural History holds 35,000 of them—I wondered how Donald Ortner found the ones with scurvy. As it happened, he discovered them through something I knew from my days at the Atwater Kent Museum: the computerized museum inventory. Every object in a museum is supposed to have a record of what it is, where it came from, and when the museum accessioned it. In times past, these records were hand-written or typed, often on index cards. As computer technology came to the fore, museum staff went back to the objects, matched them with their catalog records, and following a special coding manual, entered the data into the computer. At the Atwater Kent, this long and arduous process was in play when I was executive director in the 1990s and resulted in an excellent tool for curators to quickly locate objects for exhibitions. At the Smithsonian, it began two decades earlier and gave its researchers an essential tool for ongoing science.

In the 1970s a team of technicians was put to the task of preparing the first computer-based inventory of the National Museum of Natural History. "Whenever they saw something unusual, they would bring it to me," remembered Ortner. "The first skull I saw with bilateral lesions was of a subadult—that's what scientists call a child—from an historic period site in Alaska. I initially thought the skull showed signs of anemia, and published this result in 1984."

But, over time, Ortner began to question his own diagnosis: it didn't make sense. Anemia affects bone marrow and most often appears on the top of the skull, not the greater wing of the sphenoid, which has very little bone marrow. Even more confusing was the fact that the pits appeared on both sides of the greater wing of the sphenoid. When Ortner discovered the skull of the prehistoric Peruvian child, and found the same kind of bilateral lesions as the skull from Alaska, he showed it to Walter Putschar, a pathologist with vast knowledge. It was Putschar, now deceased, who first suggested that the Peruvian child might have suffered from scurvy.

By 1997, Ortner had found several similar cases of scurvy in skulls of subadults in archeological and anatomical museums in the Americas and Europe and, with a colleague, published an article about them. It was here that our Peruvian child made his first appearance. Two years later, Ortner and two other researchers published another article about skulls, this time focusing on those owned by the National Museum of Natural History. Using the computerized collections inventory, the scientists located 363 skulls of subadults from many archeological sites in Peru, and found evidence of scurvy in 10 percent of them. As they wrote, "Of the 36 cases of subadult scurvy where observations could be made on both sides, lesions of the greater wing of the sphenoid were bilateral in 35 individuals (97%)." Ortner had found an irrefutable way to diagnose scurvy from the skull of the prehistoric Peruvian child I held in my hands.

Ortner's discovery of scurvy is a clear instance of how lost collections become the stuff of current science. With a vast collection to mine, and the computerized inventory with which to mine it, he found new evidence in old skulls to revise his initial diagnosis. "Scientists are always finding new information. It happens in every field," said Ortner.

The field of paleopathology in which Ortner works is a subset of physical—also known as biological—anthropology, a relative newcomer in the scientific panoply, having been founded in the mid-nineteenth century. The hard truth is that its roots lie in the world of pseudoscience with a racist cast. Early physical anthropologists believed that people of different ethnic types—which they called races—showed different levels of intellectual development that was evidenced by the size of their skulls. The smaller the skull, they reasoned, the smaller the brain, and the smaller the brain, the lower the intelligence.

For more than a hundred years, the world's most distinguished physical anthropologists employed anthropometrics to determine the size of skulls of different types of people in order to rank their evolutionary status. Using beans and lead rifle shot, scales, tape measurers, and calipers, they measured the brains and skulls of women and men, thieves, murderers, and the mentally ill, members of every imaginable ethnic group, and even some long-dead scientists. What the physical anthropologists concluded time and again was that males of northern European origin represented the pinnacle of human evolutionary achievement. Since many of the physical anthropologists were males of northern European origin, this should come as no surprise.

As these pseudo-scientific findings spilled into society, they reinforced long-held prejudices and calcified them into "verifiable fact," which in turn spilled back into the world of science. The physical anthropology literature up to the 1920s and even beyond is filled with suspect hypotheses, inaccurate measurements, fudged findings, and even rigorous science based on poor data. It fueled the social philosophy of the era: segregation and miscegenation laws; eugenics, the social movement devoted to improving the human species through control of hereditary factors in mating; the theories of racial superiority that spawned the Holocaust. Sadly, signs of the theory can be found in the horrors of genocide today.

Aleš Hrdlička, the physical anthropologist who wrote the number 266599 on the skull of the Smithsonian's prehistoric Peruvian eleven-year-old, comes from this dark tradition. But although scientific racism permeated the milieu in which Hrdlička was trained and worked, he somehow avoided absorbing the worst of it, probably because he came from central, not northern, Europe. Hrdlička was born in Czechoslovakia in 1869 and lived there until age eleven, when he and his father came to America.

Hrdlička was trained as a physician, not an anthropologist. Early in his career he spent stints at the Middletown State Homeopathic Hospital for the Insane in New York and the Pathological Institute in New York because he wanted to study the anthropometrics of criminals and the insane. Between these two jobs, Hrdlička studied in Paris with Leon Manouvrier, who himself questioned the prevailing theories of his time. Manouvrier believed that nurture—social environment—rather than nature—human biology—held the secret to human variation, and he was a strong opponent of eugenics. Hrdlička carried Manouvrier's values along to the Smithsonian's National Museum of Natural History when he was appointed in 1903 as assistant curator and head of the new Division of Physical Anthropology, the first of its kind in the nation.

"Hrdlička was an excellent scientist, he never distorted the data, he let the data speak for itself," said Donald Ortner, who wrote about this pioneering physical anthropologist in an article published by the Smithsonian Institution. Hrdlička was also rude, outspoken, and opinionated; on his death, a colleague wrote: "In regard to his own conclusions Hrdlička seems to have been rarely plagued by doubts." On the positive side, he seemed to have spurned the rampant anti-Semitism of his era, and while often patronizing to women, Hrdlička did publish sixteen papers by women scientists in the *American Journal of Physical Anthropology*, the journal he founded in 1918 and which was the first of its type in the New World.

An avid collector, Hrdlička obtained skull number 266599 during a trip to Peru to collect specimens for an exposition in San Diego, California. The deal he cut with his California client enabled him to bring half of whatever he found back to the National Museum of Natural History. If Hrdlička had found it in its grave, along with other materials, the skull would have been able to be more precisely dated, and thus more scientifically valuable. Nevertheless, for Donald Ortner, there's none better, so beautifully preserved that it's easy to see scurvy's signs.

By the time Ortner began his research career at the Smithsonian in 1969 as an assistant curator in the Department of Anthropology, Hrdlička was long gone and the scientific racism that stained physical anthropology was largely a thing of the past. Ortner's focus on his peculiar specialty grew out of his interest in adaptability—how individuals adjust to the environment in which they live. Disease is an important sign of adaptability, especially over the last 10,000 years, when animal and plant domestication and agriculture led to a diet richer in calories but more limited in variety. At the same time, the human population grew and began living in greater concentrations. The more limited the diet, the more likely diseases caused by malnutrition, including scurvy, rickets, and iron deficiency anemia, will leave their evidence in bones.

Paleopathology represents a rich and vital collaboration between those who treat the living and those who study the long dead, each bringing very different training, talents, and perspectives to the task. One of the important challenges is determining the boundary between the normal and abnormal; you have to see a whole lot of bones to make a judgment call. While practicing skeletal radiologists see thousands of x-rays of individual bones from live patients, physical anthropologists see fewer skeletons but are able to track the path of disease throughout a single individual. Radiologists tend to see very sick people and so know best the most serious forms of disease, while the skeletons seen by physical anthropologists may evidence more subtle manifestations that do not always show up on a radiological film.

Most interesting from a pathogenesis perspective is the disease itself. Some diseases that physicians see in their patients have evolved over time in response to antibiotics. Because Ortner studies prehistoric human remains, he sees the baseline for a disease, the way it appeared in nature long before antibiotics and other modern methods of treatment changed its course. This remarkable symbiosis between physicians and scientists allowed paleopathology to uncover the causes of death in such diverse societies as ancient Egyptians, medieval Europeans, Native Americans, and prehistoric Peruvians.

Donald Ortner has spent his entire professional career at the National Museum of Natural History, serving as curator, departmental chair of physical anthropology, and for two years as acting director of the entire National Museum of Natural History. The museum is home to about 185 other professional scientists and the largest, most comprehensive natural history collection in the world. It is an ever expanding hoard of more than 125 million specimens of flora and fauna, rocks, minerals, meteorites, and the remains and possessions of ancient people. Established in 1910, the National Museum of Natural History is the oldest of the Smithsonian's branches and the first constructed on the north side of the National Mall. It is now joined on the Mall by others, including the National Museum of American History, the National Gallery of Art, and the Hirschhorn Museum and Sculpture Garden. A short walk away is the most recent arrival in Washington, D.C., the National Museum of the American Indian.

In 1826, when the English scientist James Smithson bequeathed his fortune of about $550,000—over $11 million in today's dollars—to "the

United States of America, to found at Washington, under the name of the Smithsonian Institution, an Establishment for the increase and diffusion of knowledge among men," he could not have imagined what his gift would spawn. The Smithsonian is a gargantuan intellectual and artistic conglomerate of sixteen museums, eight research centers, the International Exchange Service, John F. Kennedy Center for the Performing Arts, Woodrow Wilson International Center for Scholars, thousands of publications, including *Smithsonian*, a magazine for the general public, and Smithsonian Productions, which creates and manages electronic media. It's clear that the United States Congress never imagined it either. It took twenty years for Congress to accept Smithson's bequest and charter the Smithsonian Institution, because the senators and congressional representatives could not figure out what kind of vehicle was needed to realize Smithson's dauntingly broad mission.

Nothing like the Smithsonian Institution had ever been attempted before. But this was nineteenth-century America, the land of promise and unbridled optimism, where new institutional forms could be fashioned and flower.

We are all the beneficiary of Smithson's vision and Congress's acquiescence, for the place is nothing less than miraculous. This, the "nation's attic," embraces multiple forms of artistic expression and all fields of science and technology. It's a place whose myriad exhibition galleries are open free to us, the public, financed by our tax dollars, Smithson's bequest, and private sector donations and grants.

But in an institution with so sweeping an agenda, so many acres of exhibition galleries, and so many diverse interests at play, not all are created equal. If you want to find out what's important at the National Museum of Natural History, you need only compare the dreary exhibits in *Origins of Western Culture* with their neighbors down the corridor in the lavish Harry Winston Gallery, which is filled with precious jewels, including the fabulous Hope Diamond. *Origins* is the Smithsonian's exhibition about anthropology and archeology. On the day I visited, the hall was empty except for a guard who looked as bored as the life-size models of cave painters and hunter-gatherers she stood guarding.

Ortner had told me to look there for the only human skeletons on display in the entire museum. They were in a small exhibit of two tombs, circa 3100 BCE, from Bab-edh-Dhra, which is located on the east bank of the Dead Sea in Jordan. I peered through two glass windows at the recreation of the actual tombs as the archeologists had found them, complete with human bones, straw mats, and grave materials. Between the two windows were two busts modeled on the skulls inside, their hawk-nosed faces staring blankly forward. Painted on the walls were illustrations and blocks of descriptive text that looked right out of a 1960s textbook, as memorable as milk toast.

"New exhibits are very expensive," Ortner sighed. "Today they cost between $1 million and $1.5 million per 1,000 square feet. At the Smithsonian, a typical gallery is 5,000 square feet; you add it up. At this point, we can't finance new exhibits without outside support." One hopes that a future benefactor will invest the kind of money in humans that Harry Winston invested in jewels. Until then, the real action will remain behind the scenes, with Donald Ortner and his scientific colleagues.

"So, what has changed over the years for you?" I asked.

"Well, I do the same kind of work I've always done, but the methods are different, more advanced. Now we use the latest methods in radiology," he said, leading me to the room next to his with the sign "Caution—Radiation Hazard and High Voltage," on the government-beige door.

Inside was a six-foot cube lined with lead that held an x-ray machine; across the way was a CT scanner, the kind hospitals use, which looks like a metal doughnut with an x-ray tube on one side and a detector on the other. "You place your specimen here," said Ortner pointing to the bed that fit through the hole in the doughnut, "and the drum rotates as the bed slides through in tiny increments, as small as one millimeter. Each time it moves, the CT scanner takes a picture. This gives very high resolution images of tiny slices of the specimen. It is much easier to see anomalies on these images than on ones taken by a standard x-ray. And we don't have to destroy any of the specimen as we would with carbon 14 dating. The system runs off a huge computer that processes all the stuff."

The CT scanner has been used to discover the contents of a mummy bundle from the Ocean Islands, to reveal that a baboon mummy was missing the baboon that was supposed to be inside, and to observe the interior construction of a Stradivarius violin from the National Museum of American History.

But more than the technology has changed since Ortner's been on the job: there has also been a major shift in policy toward human remains. The Smithsonian Institution is subject to the repatriation provisions within the 1989 National Museum of the American Indian Act, which was passed a year before the Native Americans Graves Protection and Repatriation Act and now includes many of its policies. The act requires the Smithsonian to inventory, document, and if requested, repatriate culturally affiliated human remains, funerary objects, sacred objects, and objects of cultural patrimony of Native American and Hawaiian cultures with origins in the present-day United States. There is no comparable law governing remains from outside the United States. The skull of the prehistoric Peruvian child will remain at the Smithsonian, available to researchers long into the future.

Donald Ortner modestly demurs when asked about the relevance of his work. I'm not convinced he's right. On at least one occasion, he was front and center in a major international case, the Josef Mengele case in Brazil. Mengele was a Nazi German SS officer and a physician at Auschwitz who was known as the "Angel of Death" for the experiments he performed on camp inmates. After the war, he first hid in Germany under an assumed name, then escaped to South America. In 1986 the Simon Wiesenthal Foundation, which is dedicated to bringing former Nazis to justice, learned that Mengele might have died and been buried in Brazil. The skeleton was exhumed, but the team of experts on the case could not tell for certain whether this skeleton belonged to the evil physician.

"I was dragged in by the U.S. Department of Justice because of my expertise in skeletons and infectious disease, said Ortner frowning. "Mengele's SS records showed that he had osteomyelitis, an infection of the bone marrow, and had also fallen from a tree at about the age of fifteen and injured his hip. The skeleton showed evidence of both of these occurrences. These two factors proved that the skeleton was Mengele. This was a very sensitive case. It turned into a political nightmare: politicians demanding reports, the press calling for interviews." Over the years, Ortner has quietly consulted on a number of cases involving children who died of starvation, but he will not discuss them. It's just too painful.

But even if he never appears in a courtroom again, Ortner's paleopathology research is relevant—essential—to our understanding of the world. The future holds even greater promise. The next-generation field is paleoepidemiology, the study of the prevalence of disease through time and space. Today, a massive Global History of Health Project is building vast databases to reinterpret the entire sweep of human health in Europe from the late Paleolithic era to the early twentieth century. The scale is staggering: anatomical and pathological data on 60,000 skeletons. Health, social, economic, and environmental data from 350 different locations. Data on climatic conditions over thousands of years. When all these data are coded, entered, and cross-referenced, the Global History of Health Project will have revolutionized the study of humankind. Researchers will be able to link and mine the databases for new knowledge about such global, chronic, human conditions as trauma and violence, biological inequality, aging, and how people fared during the rise, fall, and migrations of civilizations.

It is exciting, almost overwhelming, to think that someday we may be able to view the entire sweep of disease through the millennia and around the globe. If that's not relevant, then nothing is. And it all begins with the vast collections stored in museums.

Someday we might not only be able to see a skull of a prehistoric Peruvian child with scurvy but also gain a comprehensive view of the environmental, social, and climatic conditions in which he and his family, their ancestors, and even their descendants lived and died. While this time may be distant, you can visit his home today. Pachacamac, Peru, located about twenty-five miles from Lima, is now a major tourist destination, known for its great pyramids from the Huari, Pachacamac, and Inca states. Recently, archeologists uncovered sixty-nine tombs in a multilevel gravesite rich with burial goods and human remains. Some showed signs of scurvy.

KER-FEAL

Ker-Feal
Courtesy of the Barnes Foundation

KER-FEAL

Barnes Foundation

Many people know about Albert Barnes and the Barnes Foundation's gallery, with its fabulous artworks displayed in his distinctive style. Few know about a quieter branch of the Barnes, hidden deep in the rolling farmland of Chester County, Pennsylvania, a colonial-era farm named Ker-Feal. The farmstead and the dazzling early American antiques inside it were left largely untouched for over fifty years and are only now coming to light.

"You want to see a hidden treasure?" Kimberly Camp replied when I first broached the subject. "How about a house full of them?"

Kimberly Camp, a stately African American woman with a no-nonsense demeanor, was the Barnes Foundation's first professional museum director. On a sunny September day in 2000, she and I drove the hour-long drive from the Foundation's gallery in Merion Township to Ker-Feal. A long road led through the silent landscape of fields and forests, past a garage where a caretaker lived, and up to a two-story stone building. We stepped over the threshold and entered a dark, dank room. As Camp unveiled the windows, a stunning spectacle emerged.

Every room offered up perfectly balanced compositions of early American crafts and decorative art: pine cupboards, Windsor chairs, Pennsylvania German wardrobes and wedding chests, grandfather clocks, yarn-winders, tilt-top tables. Walls were covered with mirrored sconces, wrought-iron fixtures, and weather vanes. The original colonial-era kitchen featured a dramatic ten-foot-wide fireplace hung with pots, pans, ladles, and foot warmers. Nearby, a Welsh-style open dresser displayed a colorful array of red-ware plates and a neat row of rat-tail spoons. The living room, in a later addition to the original farmhouse, was topped with ceiling rafters from a nearby 1740s barn and filled with fine examples of Queen Anne, Hepplewhite, and Chippendale furniture.

"You may want to put this on," said Camp, handing me a mask to protect against the mold. I followed her up a flight of stairs, holding tight to the original colonial-era banister. The second-floor bedrooms featured hand-hewn bedsteads draped with coverlets and quilts patterned in reds, whites, greens, and blacks. Dr. Barnes's bedroom held a dog-sized bed for Fidèle, the family dog for whom the house was named, underneath an eighteenth-century map of Fidèle's Brittany homeland. One room was assigned to Barnes's wife Laura, another to John Dewey, Barnes's intellectual mentor, and another to his friend Charles Laughton. Over the entrance to Laughton's room hung a cookie cutter shaped like the rotund actor.

We were in a time warp. It looked as if the place had not been touched for decades. Ancient wood beams showed signs of mold, spider webs draped some windows, and sunlight had faded the colors of the delicate quilts. "Before I arrived, there weren't even blinds covering the windows," said Camp. Outside, the grounds were overgrown with weeds and saplings. "Mrs. Barnes's lovely gardens look like this because there's only one caretaker and all he has is a push lawn mower and a hand rake," she explained.

It didn't take an expert to recognize the importance and scope of this stash of stuff. Standing in Ker-Feal, I decided to discover how its sorry condition and fabulous furnishings connected to Albert Barnes and his foundation.

Albert Coombs Barnes was a complicated man: a physician, pharmaceutical mogul, philosopher, art collector, and educator with a Horatio Alger life and an uncanny eye for art. He was square-jawed and sturdily built, with a high intelligence and low boiling point, and when he got angry he let loose streams of invective, in person and in print. The man was so outspoken and so obfuscating that it's easy to forget that he was also something of a visionary. Barnes supported African American causes when it was déclassé, collected art and antiques that were ahead of the curve—at least for conservative Philadelphia—and fought the establishment with a gleeful vigor that brought forward his working-class roots.

He was born in 1872, graduated from Central High, Philadelphia's most academically challenging high school, earned his M.D. from the University of Pennsylvania at age twenty, and studied philosophy, chemistry, and pharmacology at German universities. Barnes made his fortune from a drug he and his partner invented and called Argyrol, a highly effective, low-caustic, silver-based compound used by physicians worldwide to ward off eye infections in newborns. After just two years in business, Barnes and his partner had turned an investment of $1,600—about $36,000 in today's dollars—into a business with $100,000 in sales, the equivalent of $2.2 million today. A couple of years later, Barnes bought out his partner and established the new A. C. Barnes Company, which was soon producing and marketing Argyrol and other products.

By 1910 Barnes owned a wildly profitable, multinational company and a new house in Merion Township, a tony residential suburb of Philadelphia. He then decided to become an art collector. He enlisted a high school friend and artist, William J. Glackens, who began by taking Barnes to New York to tour the galleries. In 1912 Glackens went to Paris. Barnes gave him $20,000 to purchase paintings, and Glackens returned with works by Renoir, Van Gogh, Picasso, and Cezanne. Later that year, Barnes himself traveled to Europe, the first of many trips devoted to meeting the artists, purchasing their work, and studying the great masterpieces.

Over the next few years, Albert Barnes developed his intellectual and artistic interests. He studied, began to write articles about painting, and enrolled in a seminar taught by the eminent philosopher John Dewey at Columbia University. The two became lifelong friends and intellectual colleagues. Barnes also purchased works of art—lots of it. While the Impressionists and Post-Impressionists became Barnes's major foci, he also acquired African sculpture; Native American jewelry, ceramics, and textiles; Asian paintings, prints, and sculpture; medieval sculptures and manuscripts; Old Master paintings; ancient Egyptian, Greek, and Roman art; and the work of his American contemporaries, including Sloan, Avery, Prendergast, and his friend Glackens.

But Barnes wanted to be more than a collector. Based on a successful educational experiment he had launched among his factory workers, he set out to shape his dream: a school of art with his collection as its core. In 1922 the Commonwealth of Pennsylvania granted a charter to the Barnes Foundation, an educational institution dedicated to "promote the advancement of education and the appreciation of the fine arts." To address the interest of his wife Laura, the by-laws also called for the establishment of "an arboretum . . . together with a laboratory of arboriculture."

In 1925 the doors to the new gallery opened, and soon an eminent faculty was teaching aesthetics to a small cadre of specially selected students. Four years later, Albert Barnes sold his company to devote the rest of his life to the Barnes Foundation.

To those unfamiliar with Barnes's massive, dense treatise *The Art in Painting*, the twenty-three rooms of his gallery may appear as a jumble of artists, periods, and forms. In fact, they are illustrations of his pedagogy. He carefully crafted compositions of paintings, furniture, and pieces of hammered wrought iron to illustrate the continuity of form—the artists' use of light, line, color, and space—in art from different eras. These "ensembles" are not only the tools Barnes used to train students. They are also his distinctive signatures—works of art in themselves—revealing the eye of the collector.

Barnes had long been interested in early American furniture and crafts, and he included some in his art gallery. During the 1930s, as war threatened in Europe, he was forced to curtail his travels abroad and turned to collecting closer to home. His interest in Pennsylvania German antiques may have originated in his lineage: in one of the letters in the archives, he writes that his grandmother had Pennsylvania German roots.

He was well ahead of his time. Early Americana, especially the work of self-taught artists—what Barnes referred to as "primitives"—did not interest most collectors until well after the end of World War II. By 1940 he had amassed a sizable collection, and in that year he purchased a farm with a colonial farmhouse to place it in.

Ker-Feal's eight-room farmhouse was built in 1775, and as Barnes described, each room had "its original paneling, ceiling rafters, floor, window frames and glass, hardware and open fireplace." A Philadelphia architectural firm was hired to design two wings in the Colonial Revival style, constructed of local stone, to make a seamless transition from old to new. Old paneling and hardware were installed when possible, augmented with new materials, fashioned to match those in the original structure. Electricity, bathrooms, closets, and a kitchen were added to provide modern comfort. A shed and a new garage that doubled as a caretaker's cottage used materials recycled from an eighteenth-century barn located elsewhere on the property, to closely match the farmstead. Within two years, the house was completed, the furniture installed, and Albert and Laura Barnes were using Ker-Feal as a weekend retreat.

A couple of weeks after my visit to Ker-Feal, Kimberly Camp invited me to the silent, faded elegance of Laura and Albert Barnes's Merion home, which now serves as the Foundation's administrative building, to read through its original bylaws, board minutes, trust indenture, and all of the amendments to it. The tall stack of documents revealed that between 1922 and 1950, Albert Barnes amended the trust indenture ten times. During his lifetime, he would hold exclusive control over curriculum, collection, and enrollment. After his death, nothing would change. No changes to the collection and no exhibitions of work other than those owned by the Foundation would be permitted. No artworks would be sold, loaned, or copied. No fund-raising events would be allowed. Public access would be limited and "plain people" would not be charged admission. It's not unusual for institutional charters to carry restrictions, but the ones Barnes established prohibited the Foundation from raising funds or earning any income other than that generated by its endowment. He essentially froze the place in time.

In all the legal documents, there was one reference to Ker-Feal: Albert Barnes's final will and testament dated October 6, 1944. In it he states that he "undertook at Ker-Feal, a farm in Chester County, Pennsylvania, to create a living museum of art and to develop a botanical garden, both to be used as part of the educational purpose of THE BARNES FOUNDATION."

Kimberly Camp handed me a photocopy of *House and Garden* magazine dated December 1942. "You might want to take a look at this," she said. It was the most complete record of Albert and Laura Barnes's intention for Ker-Feal.

The cover featured a photo of Albert and Laura Barnes and their dog greeting the reader at the farmhouse's entrance. Inside the magazine were articles about the Foundation, the gallery, the arboretum, and Ker-Feal, with accompanying photographs. Flipping through the pages, I was struck by how carefully Ker-Feal's rooms were composed, and how similar they appeared to those I'd seen only a few weeks before. As it turned out, Ker-Feal was more than a weekend retreat; Barnes envisioned it as an extension of the Barnes Foundation, and virtually nothing had been moved for more than five decades.

"Just as the Foundation's gallery is not a museum—that is, an assemblage of relics of documentary value to historians or academics— Ker-Feal, an early American farmhouse and part of the Foundation's equipment, is not a storage house for sentimental attachments to early American life," wrote Violette de Mazia, the Foundation's director of education, in *House and Garden*. "On the contrary, in farmhouse as in gallery, the objects selected and the way they are placed in relation to each other offer material for the study of art from the point of view of the reactions of human beings to the world around them; how and in what medium these feelings are expressed."

The authentic American decorative art "represents the most important styles of furniture of the period extending from 1700 to about 1790," wrote Albert Barnes. Pennsylvania German pieces share rooms with Virginia and New England furniture "to demonstrate objectively certain principles of composition emphasized in the course of art appreciation at the Barnes Foundation."

Impressionist paintings, African sculpture, Pennsylvania German furniture and fixtures—in the eyes of Albert Barnes, art and crafts of all genres revealed the same aesthetic principles, the same expression of the artist in reaction to the world around him or her. As Barnes developed his interest and his eye, he began to collect systematically, learn more, and share his knowledge. In December 1941 he took three of his assistants to Winterthur, Henry Francis du Pont's mansion in nearby Delaware, filled with an exceptionally fine collection of early American decorative art. Barnes obtained early prototypes of European furniture that served as points of departure for American craftsmen. He lectured Barnes Foundation students on the transitions between European and American chairs.

Ker-Feal's grounds also became an extension of the Barnes Foundation's educational program. In 1940, Laura Barnes founded its Arboretum School in Merion Township, which featured a botanical garden. Once Ker-Feal's farmhouse was finished and furnished, she began transforming its landscape. As trees, shrubs, and other plants were added to the Merion garden, duplicates were often planted at

Ker-Feal. Laura Barnes constructed a formal terraced garden of roses and other perennials on soil excavated from the Barnes's swimming pool. She established a botanical garden in an eighteenth-century quartz quarry and planted a fruit orchard, a blueberry patch, and extensive flower gardens. Over time, Ker-Feal's grounds were transformed into a lush and lovely mix of formal gardens and natural plantings, local flora and rare botanical specimens. Other acreage was rented to farmers who cultivated alfalfa, barley, and other crops. Arboretum school students regularly visited as part of their classes in plant geography, geology, botany, plant propagation, plant materials, and landscape architecture.

In 1951 Albert Barnes was killed when a truck struck his car on his way back from Ker-Feal to Merion. His dog Fidèle, who was in the car, was so badly mangled that he had to be put down. It is said that Laura Barnes never spent a night at Ker-Feal again.

After Barnes's death, as stipulated in his will, Ker-Feal became part of the Barnes Foundation. Laura Barnes, who succeeded her husband as director, and Violette de Mazia, who managed the Foundation after Laura Barnes's death, allowed its art and arboretum students to visit Ker-Feal. During the 1970s, 1980s, and 1990s it was periodically open to the public for the annual Chester County Day house tours, and other small groups were permitted to visit by special appointment. But, because the Foundation was restricted from raising funds, it could not afford to maintain Ker-Feal. The buildings, remarkable furnishings, and beautiful grounds received only the minimal attention one caretaker could provide. In fact, things got worse. When the Navajo rugs at the Merion art gallery became infested with moths, they were dumped at Ker-Feal and the bugs got into the textiles.

By 1989 Violette de Mazia had died and all of the Foundation's original trustees had either died or resigned. Control passed to Lincoln University, which, under the terms of the final amendment to the Foundation's trust indenture, assumed responsibility for nominating four of its five trustees. Albert Barnes's selection of Lincoln University, an eminent black college, was in keeping with his long interest in black history and culture, his donations to African American colleges, and his role as one of America's first major collectors of African sculpture, which he displayed in the gallery. A year later, Lincoln University nominated Richard H. Glanton to the Foundation's board of trustees and he soon became its president. Glanton, a lawyer by training, sought to break Albert Barnes's indenture and bring his art to the public. Glanton battled in court with the Foundation's neighbors to dramatically expand visitation. He fought with its students to sell fifteen paintings and take other artwork on an international tour.

In the early 1990s, a court granted permission for the Barnes Foundation to mount an extraordinarily successful international tour of eighty-one masterworks. The tour generated $17 million and Glanton used $12 million of it to renovate the dilapidated Merion art gallery and install climate control and security systems. He also won the right to modestly expand gallery attendance from 500 to 1,200 visitors a week. Unfortunately, these gains cost millions in legal fees, drawn from the Foundation's already dwindling endowment. Little was left for Ker-Feal. Few beyond its neighbors even knew it existed.

In November 1998, Kimberly Camp was hired as executive director of the Barnes Foundation. She inherited responsibility for a multibillion-dollar collection housed in a starving institution. The $10 million Albert Barnes had left to the endowment in the 1920s had been almost depleted. It never grew much beyond Barnes's original gift because he restricted all investments to safe but low-interest bonds. The revenue from the art tour could not be used for operating expenses, and those costs had tripled, much of it from the utility bills associated with the new climate control and security systems.

Perhaps saddest of all, the collection was suffering from neglect. As it turned out, Albert Barnes has acquired much more than the work displayed in the gallery: approximately 2,000 objects were in storage and another 2,000 were at Ker-Feal. There was also a library and an archive of Barnes's extensive correspondence and other documents. None of it had ever been professionally catalogued, inventoried, or its condition assessed. No one knew exactly how much was there or what shape it was in.

Kimberly Camp jumped in fearlessly to untangle the knot of interconnected problems. She began mending fences with disgruntled neighbors and alienated Barnes students. She worked tirelessly to invigorate the Foundation as an educational center for students and scholars. She hired the first professional development director in the organization's history and announced its first fund-raising campaign with a goal of $85 million. Since admission to the gallery was frozen at the meager sum of $5 per person, Camp generated revenue from a museum shop, an audio tour, and a new parking lot, which was paid for by liquidating the last of the endowment.

In November 2000, the Getty Foundation awarded the Barnes Foundation a $500,000 grant to begin the first-ever comprehensive inventory and assessment of the collection. The Pew Charitable Trusts matched the Getty's gift dollar for dollar. In 2002 Camp secured a grant to begin restoration of Ker-Feal, which desperately needed a climate-control system, security, updated electricity, and mold remediation. But though she was able to attain grants for specific projects, few dollars came in for operating expenses. It's tough to raise funds for an institution with a problematic past.

At that juncture something happened that changed the entire picture. That something was a plan to save the Barnes Foundation, proposed by a team of powerful foundations, philanthropists, and government leaders. With a rapidly escalating operating deficit and a group of contentious neighbors who frowned on tour buses cluttering the streets of Merion Township, the place could not survive where it was. The Barnes Foundation's art gallery needed to move, to take its place among the tourist attractions along Philadelphia's museum mile, the Benjamin Franklin Parkway.

This bold and controversial plan would overturn Albert Barnes's trust indenture. It also meant that Lincoln University had to relinquish control over board nominations, in order to assure potential donors that the Foundation controlled its own destiny. In September 2002, the Foundation's board sought court approval to move the Merion gallery and everything in it to Philadelphia, with litigation costs covered by a $500,000 grant from the Pew Charitable Trusts. A year later, the governor of Pennsylvania pledged more than $30 million over three years to Lincoln University; a month after that, Lincoln's board voted to allow expansion of the Barnes Foundation's board from five to fifteen members, with the majority representing the public.

In December 2004, Judge Stanley Ott of the Montgomery County Orphans' Court approved the Barnes Foundation's petition to relocate from suburban Merion to downtown Philadelphia. With the help of the powerful foundations, philanthropists, and government leaders, within eighteen months there were pledges of $150 million to build the new Barnes and seed an endowment to care for it.

Following the Barnes Foundation's story in the newspapers, I knew Kimberly Camp had resigned as of December 2005. I began to wonder how Ker-Feal fit into these ambitious plans. I'd heard rumors that art dealers and real estate developers had been snooping around Ker-Feal. Would the property and its contents be sold to pay for the grand new gallery on the Benjamin Franklin Parkway?

I called the Foundation and received a call back from Barbara Buckley, head of conservation, who agreed to show me around Ker-Feal. For the second time, I drove through Chester County's rolling hills, noticing that lavish new mansions stood where farmland used to be.

"Albert Barnes had a conservator on staff, which was unusual at the time," Barbara Buckley told me on the hot August day in 2006 when she met me at Ker-Feal. "I'm the first full-time conservator on staff since the 1950s." Buckley was managing a team of eight conservators and art handlers as part of a massive collections assessment project. The $3 million foundation-funded effort also included registrars, archivists, and thirty-four consulting curators. The size of the team reflected not only the importance but also the scale of the collections: 2,000 linear feet of archival documents and 9,000 works of art, spanning the centuries from 2350 BCE up to Barnes's death in 1951.

Barbara Buckley escorted me into the farmhouse. The dankness and darkness were gone, replaced by the cool buzz of air conditioners and fans. Soft light filtered through the window blinds. The rooms, with their wrought-iron hinges, pewter objects, glass sconces, wooden tables and chairs, and hutches banked with red-ware pottery appeared the same, but somehow different. The place looked occupied, fresh, clean; the smell of mold was gone.

"Ker-Feal was built over a spring, which is one of the reasons that the mold grew so extensively," explained Buckley. "After installing a new air conditioning system and adding fans to keep the air circulating, we vacuumed the interior walls, ceilings, and floors with a high efficiency HEPA vacuum that filters out mold spores. The walls were then washed with a solution of bleach and water and rinsed with distilled water."

"A lot of people are working on this project," I said. "What do they all do?"

"The registrars took the first step. They inventoried all collections objects: the furniture, ceramics, metalwork, and textiles," she said, handing me a red notebook. Its pages were covered with notes on each object, some with digital photos inserted next to the text.

The next step was to catalog the objects and research provenance. With a grant from the National Endowment for the Arts, the Foundation was able to catalog and photograph 260 pieces of red-ware pottery, and it turned up important new information.

"We now know, for example, that Barnes collected not just American pottery and metalwork, but also pieces from Europe," Buckley explained, pointing out five large serving plates propped up on the mantle. "The two on the left are English, the two on the right are Carolina Moravian, and the large one in the middle with Adam and Eve in the Garden of Eden is from Germany. Unlike many collectors who only want the best items, the ones used for special occasions, Barnes also collected pieces that people used every day." She pointed to the old wooden hutch on her left, banked with rows of smaller plates, brick red with bright yellow squiggles and lines.

"Conservators look at the condition of the objects. We're concerned about the environment in which the objects live; it's important that the environment is monitored, which includes housekeeping, to prevent infestations of insects and mold. The temperature and humidity must remain steady. The lighting has to be safe: high levels with too much ultraviolet light will fade paper and textiles."

We walked into the original farmhouse kitchen. I pulled out the photocopy of the *House and Garden* magazine that Kimberly Camp had handed me six years before. "The red-ware pottery in the hutch looks pretty much the same," I said, looking closer, "though some pieces have been moved."

"Well, remember the *House and Garden* article is from 1942. Albert Barnes lived until 1951, so he did move some things around. This is how the hutch looked the day he died," said Buckley, handing me a photograph. "Soon after he died, the Foundation hired a photographer to record every room."

I held it up to the hutch; the picture and arrangement matched. On my first visit to Ker-Feal in 2000, I'd felt like I was in a time warp. I was.

I thought about Laura Barnes, living with a cantankerous husband who didn't want anything moved. "Do you ever imagine what it would

CHAPTER 6

have been like to live in this house with Dr. Barnes?" I asked. "It must have been stifling, to have to live around his collection."

"No, he lived *with* his collection, not *around* it," Buckley replied. She thought for a moment. "Remember, Barnes's educational philosophy was that art should be part of everyday life. At Ker-Feal, Barnes lived his educational program."

"Where are the textiles?" I asked, looking around for the rugs and quilts I remembered from six years before.

"Ah, the textiles," sighed Buckley. "The textiles are not in good condition."

She led me up a flight of stairs and into Laura Barnes's bedroom. Her cozy room had been transformed into a textile conservation workroom with a HEPA filtered vacuum, rolls of plastic, and other supplies. A plastic cocoon sealed with tape lay on a worktable.

"The rugs, towels, quilts, and other fabrics were infested with tiny cream-colored moths which, in their larva stage, eat through wool and silk. We wrapped each piece in tissue, then in a plastic cocoon, sealed it with duct tape, then wrapped and sealed it again. The double layer of plastic is to protect the fabric inside from condensation during the freezing process. We took the textiles to a freezer truck at a freezer warehouse. The wrapped textiles were placed in the truck, where the temperature was minus five degrees Fahrenheit. They stayed there for five days. After they thawed, we unwrapped and vacuumed them. There are other ways to kill moths but we wanted to do it in a chemical-free way."

"Why was Ker-Feal abandoned for so long?" I asked, remembering I asked Kimberly Camp the same question six years earlier.

"It wasn't abandoned," Buckley explained. "Mrs. Barnes came out periodically until she died. There was always a caretaker living here. But the priorities were clearly elsewhere."

"The priorities were elsewhere," I repeated. "Has that really changed? Now the priority is building the new gallery in Philadelphia. Given this, what do you think will happen to Ker-Feal?"

"While the current focus is on the new art gallery, Ker-Feal isn't being ignored," she said. "The arboretum school continues to use Ker-Feal, and teachers in the art program are beginning to bring their students. The conservation work continues. And, there's talk about displaying

98

some items from Ker-Feal in the new gallery in Philadelphia. But we who care about Ker-Feal have to take a longer view."

I thought about this. Curators and conservators are concerned about preservation, saving things for posterity. They have to take the longer view.

"When you're in the Merion gallery, the paintings are often the focus," she continued. "But Barnes's educational philosophy encourages us to see art in everyday life. Ker-Feal shows this. I do believe it will be open to the public someday."

There are high hopes for the Barnes Foundation. Derek Gillman, its new president, is an inspired choice, for in his prior position as president of the Pennsylvania Academy of the Fine Arts, he oversaw both a museum and a school. The Foundation's board has pledged to preserve the buildings in Merion Township, the arboretum and its school, and Ker-Feal. The new gallery in Philadelphia will continue the art education program. It will present Barnes's signature ensembles and make them available to millions more visitors.

But while the parts of the Barnes Foundation's suburban gallery will be replicated, the experience will never be the same. The smell and feel, the intimacy and surprise, the singular and memorable experience of viewing Albert Barnes's collection in the space he created for it will be lost forever.

In fact, when the gallery moves to Philadelphia, Ker-Feal will become more important: the only place left to experience Albert Barnes's masterful and distinctive compositions intact and *in situ*. It's slated to become what Barnes envisioned, a living history museum. At the time of Barnes's death, Ker-Feal housed over 2,000 objects: furniture, glass, textiles, iron, tin, brass, and copper, and—according to one expert—the world's largest and most complete collections of early rural red-ware. All will remain in the signature ensembles he left on the day he died.

It may be years before the building is sufficiently stabilized to open it to the public on a regular basis. The floors won't carry the weight of groups of visitors. But we, like Barbara Buckley, must take the longer view.

Six years and a few million dollars can make a world of difference. Ker-Feal has recently been added to the National Register of Historic Places, which assures its survival. The Commonwealth of Pennsylvania has recently certified the Foundation's art education program. The faded elegance of its administration building remains, but it is no longer silent. Now staff members are at work there, including three in the library and archives who are available to help researchers locate original documents. Curatorial information and thousands of digital images and photographs have been entered into a new electronic catalog, allowing users to search and access the collections. The strictures of the trust indenture that bound the Foundation for decades have been deviated from, but with that departure the institution is now free to follow a vital new course, one that will bring its treasures to millions more of the "ordinary people" whom Albert Barnes cared most about.

Barnes died before his intentions for Ker-Feal could be realized; the constraints he placed over the finances of his foundation left little to properly care for it. But, if you think about it, this benign neglect might have saved the place. If people had known about it and visited it in its fragile state, Ker-Feal could have been destroyed. Despite the light, dust, moths, and mold, it survived and much can be restored. Not today, but certainly in the future, we will be able to experience Ker-Feal as Barnes himself lived it.

How would the cantankerous Albert Barnes feel about all this? We'll never know because he's long dead. What we do know is that the Barnes Foundation can now evolve, change, and assume its place in the American cultural firmament. Its story isn't over. It's only beginning a new chapter.

PLAN FOR THE DOME OF THE UNITED STATES CAPITOL

Plan for the Dome of the U.S. Capitol, 1855, Thomas Ustick Walter, Architect
Courtesy of the Athenaeum of Philadelphia

PLAN FOR THE DOME OF THE UNITED STATES CAPITOL

Athenaeum of Philadelphia

One of the architect Thomas Ustick Walter's drawings for the United States Capitol building is a beautifully rendered cross-section of its dome, the left side showing the interior skeleton, the right its exterior skin. The massive scale and meticulous detail make it a masterpiece of architectural illustration, but what's even more remarkable is that it exists at all. The drawing was moved from the Washington home of its architect to Philadelphia, and after his death to Baltimore, and following Walter's wife's death, transported across the country, where it was squirreled away in a bunkhouse on a Colorado ranch for almost seventy-five years, and then narrowly escaped a tornado.

Thomas Ustick Walter was the most influential architect of mid-nineteenth-century America. Walter essentially invented the architectural profession in America. He taught architecture to students, edited architecture books for the building industry, lectured on architecture before the general public, and had the idea for the American Institute of Architects. He survived two bankruptcies, fathered thirteen children with two wives, and died almost broke. Despite his significance and fascinating life, Walter is largely unknown outside the field of architectural history. Until Roger Moss, executive director of the Athenaeum of Philadelphia, showed me Walter's *Plan for the Dome of the United States Capitol*, I'd never heard of him. But, with Moss as guide, I was soon on a journey that stretched from the early days of American architecture through the strife of the Civil War and up to today.

"Here's Thomas Ustick Walter and his two wives," said Moss pointing to three portraits that hung in the hallway outside his antique-filled office. We stopped before the Byronesque-handsome man with dark, compelling eyes flanked by two ladies in Victorian finery. I had gone to visit this distinguished author and authority on architectural history to learn how he had been able to transform a decrepit private lending library into one of the nation's most revered historical archives. "Though Walter lost the commission to design the Athenaeum of Philadelphia to another architect, he designed many buildings, including the two most important of his era: Founder's Hall at Girard College in Philadelphia and the expansion of the United States Capitol in Washington, D.C." Moss led me past the paintings and down a flight of stairs to the storage vaults below.

The space was a curator's paradise, so clean you could eat off the floor. The 5,000-square-foot complex was lined with metal racks of rare books and compression-stacked cabinets that maximize use of space. Every cabinet was stacked with drawers; every drawer filled with documents, prints, and photographs. Every item was·catalogued, conserved, and tucked snugly away. I took a sniff: none of the musty odor that's common where old books and papers are stored. Roger Moss had created a pristine, museum-quality, climatically stable storage vault in the basement of a mid-nineteenth-century building. This was no easy accomplishment, as I knew from our struggles to stabilize the dicey environmental conditions in the Atwater Kent Museum, a structure from around the same period. "Millions of dollars have been spent to keep the room dry," said Moss dryly.

Historical archives such as the Athenaeum of Philadelphia, like museums, are collecting institutions, but the things they own and the way they operate are a bit different from their more publicly focused counterparts. While museums collect two- and three-dimensional objects, archival collections are strictly two-dimensional: family, business, and institutional records, photographs, and prints. Their primary functions are to preserve these documents and to service the researchers who use them. The call to serve the public is not as loud. In fact, there's nothing loud about an archive. You'll never see a busload of schoolchildren or tourists in funny shirts visiting the Athenaeum of Philadelphia, even though it's less than a block from Independence Hall. It's not even open on weekends, when most tourists are around. Instead, if you go—and you must go on a weekday—you're likely to find a couple of scholars examining documents, a couple of members borrowing books, and a staff of helpful people busy helping them in the hush of the building's two grand reading rooms.

Roger Moss pulled out the wide metal drawer to reveal Walter's *Plan for the Dome of the Unites States Capitol.* The huge illustration, forty-two inches wide, fifty-four inches high, is dated 1855, but it looks fresh off the architect's desk. "It was originally bound in a decaying leather binding, glued on acidic paper—in terrible shape," said Moss. "We had the drawing removed, de-acidified, cleaned, repaired, and encapsulated in Mylar. This kind of preservation is expensive, but we're dealing here with a national treasure."

"If the cross-section is a national treasure, why is it hidden in storage?" I asked.

Moss looked surprised by the question. "Just because it's stored in the vault doesn't mean it's hidden," he explained. "It's always available to researchers. Though it's been exhibited here a number of times and loaned for shows at other eminent institutions, including the Library of Congress, the rendering will never be placed on permanent display. Works on paper are very fragile and light will fade the colors if they are exhibited for too long."

An eminent but unknown architect whose work deserves the finest of care. Suddenly, I wanted to know more about Thomas Ustick Walter.

Born in Philadelphia in 1804, Walter was bitten by the architecture bug early. Later in life he described his early education as "liberal but not collegiate," but in fact, years before colleges offered architectural programs, Walter assembled one for himself. He learned construction techniques and bricklaying while apprenticing at his father's successful construction business. He learned architectural drawing and project management while apprenticing in the office of his master and mentor, William Strickland, a client of his father and one of America's best and first native-born architects. Walter studied Euclidean geometry with a retired sea captain and landscape painting in watercolors from a practicing artist—both essential for architectural presentation drawings. To top off his training, Walter enrolled as one of the first students in America's first technical institute, the Franklin Institute, and mastered mathematics, physics, architectural theory, and mechanical construction. By age twenty-five, the ambitious young man had assembled the basic ingredients of what would eventually become the standard university-level architectural course. He was ready to reach for his dream.

This dream was to become first among the handful of professional architects practicing in the United States. America's first architect, Benjamin Latrobe, who arrived in Philadelphia in 1799, trained William Strickland, and Strickland trained Walter.

Once he mastered his profession, things moved quickly for young Walter. In 1829, he established his own practice. During his second year in business, he scored his first plum assignment: designing and supervising the construction of the Philadelphia County Prison, called Moyamensing, a job he likely secured with the help of his politically connected father. Walter designed a gigantic Gothic castle, complete with battlements, turrets, and pointed archways. The acclaim he received encouraged him to compete for the most prestigious commission of his day: Girard College for Orphans.

On his death, Stephen Girard, America's first multimillionaire, had left millions to the city of Philadelphia to build a home for white fatherless boys. The commission was an architect's dream: a virtually unlimited budget to create a magnificent tribute to public philanthropy. Walter offered up a lavish design of highest French elegance, and beat out scores of architects, including his mentor, William Strickland, in the national competition.

It was during the Girard commission that Walter earned his stripes as an architect, for the structure he created became the nation's most important neoclassical building. Walter was guided by the chairman of the building committee, Nicholas Biddle, president of the Second Bank of the United States, who was enamored with the architecture of classic Greece as the embodiment of democracy. Soon Biddle persuaded the young architect to trade French elegance for Greek antiquity, and a remarkably brief eleven days later, Walter delivered a new drawing for Girard College's Founders Hall, a magnificent Greek temple.

The commission gained Walter a national reputation, but, as many architects have learned, reputation alone can't pay the bills. In 1837, America suffered a major bank panic, which, along with the depression that followed, stopped all new construction cold. Walter, along with many of his customers, went bankrupt. All work on Girard College ceased, and in 1843, to make ends meet, Walter accepted a commission to design and construct a breakwater for a harbor in Venezuela. He spent more than a year on the job before returning to Philadelphia and completing Girard College in 1848, fifteen years after he had secured the job. The $2 million budget made Girard College the single most expensive building in the United States up to the Civil War.

By 1850, Walter's business had recovered, and he had become Philadelphia's leading architect. In that year alone this workaholic's output included seventeen houses, four stores, twelve churches, five schools, two hotels, and two county government projects. That year he also secured the only commission that could top Girard College: the expansion of the United States Capitol in Washington, D.C. The assignment was to add two wings to the original building in order to accommodate the growing number of senators and congressional representatives from the newly created states. Walter designed the wings, then went the next step and persuaded Congress that a majestic new cast-iron dome was needed to balance the proportions of the expanded Capitol.

Roger Moss and I looked down at Walter's *Plan for the Dome of the United States Capitol*. "The left side, the interior view, shows Walter's engineering prowess," Moss said. Walter created a cast-iron skeleton and wrapped it with two cast-iron domes, one for the exterior and one for the interior. Both domes were bolted to cast-iron cantilevers to suspend them in space. Bricks and masonry held the skeleton in place, carrying its weight to the ground.

We looked at the right side of the cross-section, the one showing the exterior of the dome. "This illustrates Walter's aesthetic ability," said Moss. The exterior of the Capitol dome features as elegant an array of columns, brackets, and rosettes as you'd find on any stately building of the time—but with an important difference. Instead of using the traditional materials of stone or wood, Walter's dome is made of cast iron, painted limestone gray to match the structure below.

At the time, cast iron was state of the art. By using it, Walter was able to create a dome of twice the size of its predecessor, but only 20 percent heavier, with hundreds of windows and a skylight to add light and ventilation to the great rotunda below. With cast iron, the workers could also expedite construction, since multiple pieces could be replicated quickly from a single mold. Cast iron is fireproof, an especially useful attribute for those living in the 1800s, when cities were prone to fires. In fact, its safety benefit proved a salient selling point to the members of Congress, who quickly approved Walter's design when he showed them his beautiful rendering.

Walter knew that his dome would work, since his research was as meticulous as his design. During a London trip to prepare for the Girard College assignment, he had spent a stormy night high atop St. Paul's cathedral, examining how its metal roof conducted electricity. What Walter could not have imagined was the lasting influence of his design. His dome transformed the United States Capitol into America's most famous man-made landmark.

An achievement like Walter's would have been exceptional in the best of times; in the one in which he found himself, it was nothing less than miraculous. As workers were casting small pieces of the dome on the grounds of the Capitol and building the structure, the Civil War was raging just across the Potomac River in Virginia. Though Congress cut off payment for construction of the Capitol until the hostilities ended, Walter and his patriotic crew continued to work throughout the Civil War. An 1861 photograph of Abraham Lincoln's inauguration owned by the Athenaeum shows the president standing in front of a half-built, open-topped Capitol ringed in scaffolding.

The war could not have been easy for Walter, whose sons fought for both the North and the South. Moreover, the climate of war made the practice of architecture problematic. A letter dated May 3, 1861, from Walter to his wife noted that 4,000 Union soldiers were bivouacked in the Capitol. "The building is like one great water closet—every hole and corner is defiled—one of the capitol police says there are cart loads of ____ in the dark corners," complains Walter. The blank was part of Walter's letter; a Victorian gentleman would never write the unpleasant word that's obviously missing. "These are nasty things to talk to a lady about, but ladies ought to know to what vile uses the most elegant things are devoted in times of war."

On May 31, 1865, a month and a half after Lincoln's death, Walter resigned his post and returned to his family in Philadelphia's Germantown neighborhood. He had suffered through fourteen years on the job, five during the Civil War, and a government supervisor who tried to steal credit for his work. Despite this, Walter completed not only the expansion and dome of the Capitol but also a remarkably ambitious schedule of fourteen other federal buildings. These included design and construction supervision of St. Elizabeth's Hospital for the Insane and major additions to the Patent Office and United States Treasury.

It was here that Walter's story took a turn. As he left Washington to return home, he packed up the *Plan for the Dome of the United States Capitol*, and the diaries, correspondence, and other records that documented his entire career, particularly those years in Washington. It turned out that the government was unwilling to pay Walter anything over and above the salary he received for his original assignment for the Capitol wings. He received no money for his work on St. Elizabeth's Hospital, none for the Patent Office or Treasury, and none for his extraordinary Capitol dome.

Walter and his large family desperately needed the money. He had looked forward to spending his declining years in retirement, but a string of bad investments had wiped out his savings. Walter carried on the campaign to secure payment for his work for the rest of his life. When he died, his widow and children moved, along with the rendering of the dome and Walter's other documents, to Baltimore so they could be closer to Washington and continue the quest for payment. Finally, in 1899, Congress awarded Walter's heirs $14,000, a small fraction of the sum by all rights due to him.

"How did the drawing get to the Athenaeum?" I asked Roger Moss, as we stood in the Athenaeum's crypt.

"Go visit Robert Ennis," said Moss. "He's the expert on Thomas Walter. He'll tell you more."

Robert Ennis fell in love with Walter's Girard College one spring day in 1970. At the time, he was a graduate student in architectural history in search of a topic for his doctoral dissertation. Ennis soon learned that he had no hope of completing the dissertation and securing his Ph.D. unless he could find Walter's papers and designs for the Capitol. They had been missing for almost a hundred years.

One day while on a research trip to Washington, Ennis happened upon a list of Thomas Ustick Walter's descendants. It was sitting on the desk of the architect of the U.S. Capitol. "I wrote letters to every name on the list, describing my research project, and requesting any papers or memorabilia in family hands," Ennis told me. "While some family members responded, the most important person did not: Isabel Becker, Walter's great-granddaughter. She owned the lion's share of Walter papers but had shunned all requests to share them."

On a gloomy February night in 1972, Robert Ennis went to bed despondent. Without the papers being available to scholars, Walter, the great architect, would be lost to time. Suddenly the phone rang and a voice told him, "This is Isabel Becker. Yes, you can come to see my great-grandfather's things."

Robert Ennis wasted no time. The following week he and his partner were on a plane to Denver. They rented a car and drove to a thousand-acre ranch in the foothills of the Rocky Mountains where Isabel Becker, her daughter, and granddaughter were raising quarter horses and German shepherd dogs. Isabel Becker was living in a former cowboy bunkhouse that she had renovated into a snug home. When she opened the door to welcome her guest, Robert Ennis remembered, "I began to cry."

Isabel Becker's bunkhouse was filled with her great-grandfather's treasures. Over the fireplace, in a place of honor, hung an 1855 watercolor of the east front of the Capitol, sporting its new wings and dome. On the wall to the left was the final perspective of Founder's Hall at Girard College. Framing a doorway was the portrait of Thomas Walter's second wife and Brumidi's oil sketch for *The Apotheosis of George Washington*, the fresco that now wraps the interior of the Capitol dome, depicting the first president of the United States rising into clouds in glory. Bookcases were crammed with Walter's papers. Hundreds of drawings by Walter, Strickland, and other architects of the era were stuffed in two huge boxes.

Nearby was the ranch house in which Isabel's daughter and granddaughter lived. It was filled with silver, paintings, and other family heirlooms. The rich trove was a dream come true: the materials Ennis needed to complete his dissertation. Ennis gained permission to duplicate the piles of fragile documents, and over the next few days he kept local microfilm cameras and copy machines buzzing. "I spent the next year unscrambling the mass of information for the dissertation," said Ennis.

A few months later, I joined Congresswoman Allyson Y. Schwartz, five of her favored constituents, and an official guide on a VIP tour of the capitol dome. Congressional offices, I learned, could host these. The 300 steep steps wind through the mountainous shaft between the exterior of the inside dome and the interior of the outside dome. Huge metal cantilevers span the space, bolting the two domes together. We climbed, and climbed some more, then stopped at a platform; the guide led us through a door and onto the narrow balcony that rings the interior dome. Above my head rose Brumidi's 4,664-square-foot fresco, *The Apotheosis of George Washington*, with a serene and seated George Washington surrounded by clouds, stars, and angels. Holding my breath, I bent carefully over the parapet and stared down past the coffered ceiling, painted frieze, multiple windows, and stately columns, to the floor of the Capitol rotunda some 160 feet below. Tiny tourists with cameras flashing and heads tipped back stared up at me.

We reentered the shaft between the structures and continued the ascent. The steps grew steeper, into a ladder. Holding tight to the rail, we climbed over the top of the interior dome and up to another landing. The guide opened a door, and a shock of wind hit as we crossed the threshold to outside. Federal Washington swept far below as I cautiously circled the catwalk, looking down at the Mall, Washington Monument, the Tidal Basin and Potomac River, and Union Station, webbed by streets and avenues.

There's nothing like standing on top of the dome of the United States Capitol to understand why it's important to preserve the rendering that persuaded Congress to finance it. It was time to learn how Ennis's discovery inspired a new course for the Athenaeum.

The Athenaeum of Philadelphia is one of the loveliest buildings in Philadelphia, a stately Italianate structure faced in soft shades of brownstone. Within this pristinely restored National Historic Landmark are rooms decorated with statuary, paintings, antique furniture, and decorative art. Walls are covered with bold Victorian wallpaper, floors with lush carpets. That wasn't always the case. At various times, the building had housed a mish-mash of tenants: the Board of Controllers of Public Schools, the Historical Society of Pennsylvania, the national offices of the Victorian Society in America, offices for attorneys and an insurance company, and storage for some of its members. It was home to the Philadelphia branch of the American Institute of Architects when Thomas Ustick Walter was its president. It struggled for decades to make ends meet.

By 1968, when Roger Moss was hired as secretary and librarian, the building was a disaster waiting to happen. The roof leaked and the safety and security systems were essentially dysfunctional. Some plumbing predated the First World War; the electrical system was from 1923, the furnaces from the 1950s. When a piece of cornice molding fell off the exterior and onto the pavement below, the board of directors finally faced facts: their precious lending library could not meet the city's building codes. The board and Roger Moss decided not only to bring the building up to code, but also to reach for the best. Their Athenaeum was going to be technically state-of-the-art and restored to its original 1847 glory.

With no prior experience in fund-raising, this was a bold, some would say audacious, decision by Moss and the board. But, dollar by dollar, they assembled a multimillion-dollar restoration fund from private foundations and old Philadelphia families. In 1975 Moss launched a complete mechanical overhaul, replacing dated systems with new ones: central heating, air conditioning, rest rooms, security, and lighting. Over time, steel was introduced to support the structure and bring it up to code. The basement was dug out and transformed into a world-class storage vault for rare books and drawings. Special systems were installed to achieve the constant seventy-degree Fahrenheit temperature and fifty-degree humidity needed to kill the mold that rots organic materials like paper and leather bookbindings.

With the bones in place, it was time to make the building beautiful. Experts were hired to restore its original grandeur. A master painter from England was retained to grain bookcases and woodwork to replicate oak, and to paint pillars and columns in delicious shades of white and vanilla custard, veined with butterscotch, to replicate the finest Sienna marble.

A new public gallery was installed in the first floor front, and in 1978 Roger Moss invited Robert Ennis to curate an exhibit of the work of Thomas Ustick Walter. Soon Ennis and Moss were on their way to the Colorado ranch of Walter's great-granddaughter. Turning on their substantial charm, they persuaded Isabel Becker to loan her great-grandfather's drawings for the show. Robert Ennis flew back to Philadelphia, picked up his partner, and drove west to Becker's Colorado ranch. With a tornado threatening, they quickly loaded a number of Walter's drawings into a van and drove them back east to Philadelphia. The show was a huge success.

Eventually, Isabel Becker and her daughter sold Walter's portrait, the portraits of his two wives, 150 photographs of the Capitol, 550 original drawings—including 150 of the Capitol and the *Plan for the Dome of the United States Capitol*—to the Athenaeum of Philadelphia. With some 30,000 papers—Walter was as meticulous in his record keeping as he was in his renderings—it is the most comprehensive collection from any architect before the twentieth century. It was also the first collection ever purchased by the Athenaeum, and it set the institution in a new direction. Today it is the principal repository in the region for the records of architectural achievement prior to 1945. Its holdings include 200,000 architectural drawings, more than 350,000 photographs, and extensive manuscripts representing the work of approximately 2,500 American architects. While the collection is national in scope, its principal focus is Philadelphia, a singularly important center of architecture for more than two centuries.

"Because many buildings fail to survive over time, we can only know the richness of our architectural heritage through photographs, drawings, and documents," explained Roger Moss. "Many of these would have been destroyed if we hadn't gotten in the rescue business. Other institutions had turned down collection after collection of architectural materials. When we received a call from a potential donor, we sent out trucks the very next day and the trucks returned filled with great and important work."

I looked around Moss's office, at the Victorian wallpaper, the lavish furniture, fixtures, and fittings. "How did you do it?" I asked. "What's the secret to the Athenaeum's success?"

"Focus," he said, frowning. "You've got to remain focused. There are many distractions, many opportunities. Many organizations add new programs without the funds to sustain them. That doesn't happen here. We do not rely on public money. We don't dip into the corpus of our modest endowment. We finance our organization with the proceeds from the endowment, and never draw out more than 5 percent of the corpus per year. Most importantly, our 1,500 members are very generous. They pay their annual dues and many contribute beyond that."

"This region has 350 historic sites, museums, and historical societies; a huge number," he continued. "Many are not historically significant; they have no professional expertise and no base of support. Some will die because of limited resources. It's sad, but true."

Aha, I thought. There's the answer. The Atwater Kent Museum's endowment was tiny; over a third of the budget came from government. Our exceptionally creative staff was always inventing exceptionally creative programs, launched by foundation grants. When the grants ran out, as they inevitably do, there was nothing to sustain the programs. There was a lesson in Roger Moss's fiscal prudence.

Unfortunately, Thomas Ustick Walter was not fiscally prudent. In 1873 he declared bankruptcy for the second time, shut the door on the small architectural practice that was financing his retirement, and sold the Germantown home he loved. To make ends meet, the most influential American architect of the mid-nineteenth century was forced to accept a job as a draftsman for the Pennsylvania Railroad. A year later, one of his former apprentices, John McArthur Jr., who had secured the commission for Philadelphia City Hall, appointed Walter as consulting architect. While Walter received no official credit, architectural historians will tell you that his signature is all over the building. Walter remained on the job until two weeks before his death at age eighty-three, ending a remarkable fifty-seven-year career.

"Walter's obituaries referred to him only as a draftsman, but nationally the profession mourned," said Robert Ennis, his most fervent admirer.

Ennis's story ends on a poignant note. After retrieving the great architect's massive archive from the Colorado bunkhouse and spending years mining it, Ennis faced the sad realization that he would never complete Walter's biography. Ennis never secured the Ph.D. he had tried so hard to attain. While a number of scholars have written parts of Walter's tale, his entire story has yet to be told.

Neither Thomas Ustick Walter nor Robert Ennis, who unearthed Walter's possessions after a hundred years of obscurity, accomplished all they may have wished. But both left their marks.

Walter's buildings can still be seen on the streets of historic Philadelphia, a short walk from the Athenaeum of Philadelphia. On Third Street between Spruce and Locust stand the three brownstone houses Walter designed in the late 1840s for the great furniture maker Michel

Bouvier, an ancestor of former First Lady Jacqueline Bouvier Kennedy. Across Third is Walter's doorway for Old St. Paul's Church, now the home of Episcopal Community Services. Two blocks up Spruce Street, between Fourth and Fifth, is the Baptist church where Walter worshipped, taught Sunday school, and met his second wife; its façade now fronts Society Hill Synagogue. Farther west on Spruce between Seventh and Eleventh streets stand a number of Walter's designs: a Roman Catholic orphanage, two rows of townhouses, and the doorway to the home of Nicholas Biddle, his most important patron.

With a computer, you can also visit Walter on the website of the Athenaeum of Philadelphia. With only one small gallery, almost all of its holdings have been hidden from view. Now, through digital technology, you can tour its 2004 exhibit, *Thomas Ustick Walter: Historic Architecture for a Modern World*. Or you can press a few buttons and enter the website of the Philadelphia Architects and Buildings Project, an online interactive database of architectural and historical information, biographies, and 110,000 images that link to other repositories. The website is a national model—Roger Moss would settle for nothing less—with virtual technology bringing priceless documents out of storage drawers and into the world beyond.

I've become a member of the Athenaeum of Philadelphia and often stop by to borrow books and visit Thomas Ustick Walter. Seeing his portrait in its place of honor across the hall from Roger Moss's office, it's easy to imagine how this consummate professional would feel about the consummate professionalism devoted to perpetual care of his work. The man who gave his life to the pursuit and popularization of architecture would be pleased that his papers continue to be mined by scholars and architects, and that his renderings continue to be displayed in exhibits, both actual and virtual.

Robert Ennis's legacy is also at the Athenaeum. It's in the detailed research notes he complied and the thousands of possessions of the architect he rediscovered. When Walter's definitive biography is finally written, Robert Ennis, the young student who reclaimed the *Plan for the Dome of the United States Capitol*, will surely be a part.

JOHN BROWN'S PIKE

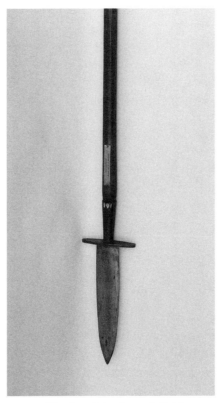

Pike from John Brown's Raid
Courtesy of the Civil War and Underground Railroad Museum of Philadelphia

JOHN BROWN'S PIKE

Civil War and Underground Railroad Museum of Philadelphia

Three men lay on the floor of the fire engine house of the federal armory in Harpers Ferry, Virginia, one dead, the others groaning in pain in the chilled black night. A large cache of pikes, long steel-tipped spears, stood propped in the corner. Four raiders and eleven prisoners watched as an exhausted old man paced back and forth, muttering to himself. "Gentlemen," he turned and said, "if you knew of my past history, you would not blame me for being here. I went to Kansas a peaceable man, and the proslavery people hunted me down like a wolf. I lost one of my sons there."

As dawn broke on the morning of October 18, 1859, the raiders took their places at the wall, peered through the gun holes, and looked straight into the eyes of a company of the United States Marine Corps carrying bayonets and sledgehammers. Suddenly, the marines rushed forward, tore open the thick oak doors, and, stepping over the dead and wounded, swarmed inside. A young lieutenant lifted his dress sword, struck the kneeling old man to the floor, and beat him unconscious. John Brown's raid on Harpers Ferry—the spark that ignited the American Civil War—was over.

Flash-forward almost 150 years to a townhouse museum in downtown Philadelphia where a volunteer has just handed me a seven-foot-long wooden rod tipped with a wicked ten-inch steel blade. It has been stored in the basement because the only case large enough to hold it was used for something else.

The townhouse was packed with stories. Stories about those who fought in the Civil War, the most wrenching conflict this nation has ever known. Stories about Philadelphia's largely unrecognized role in the war effort. Stories about the more recent battle fought to save this museum's precious relics for Philadelphia. All of these stories live on in what might be the most significant and least-known museum in a city overflowing with them—the Civil War and Underground Railroad Museum of Philadelphia.

If you've never heard of this institution (by its current name or by its two previous names, the Civil War Library and Museum and the War Library and Museum of the Military Order of the Loyal Legion of the United States), you're not alone. Few beyond the scholar and Civil War buff know it exists. It was tough to locate among the other townhouses that line this residential street; the only identification was a tarnished plaque on the façade with the inscription "U.S. Commandery-in-Chief" and the "Commandery of the State of Penna." But those who entered found themselves in a Civil War buff's heaven, albeit a claustrophobic heaven.

Top to bottom, wall to wall, the townhouse museum overflowed with relics, documents, paintings, photographs, and books donated by some of the very people who fought the war: Union officers and their descendants. Four floors were packed with scale models of battle scenes, bullet-filled tree stumps, canteens, and swords. Walls were papered with recruitment posters, flags, and battlefront paintings. Along the steep and narrow stairway hung the nation's largest collection of military escutcheons, velum documents printed or hand-lettered and decorated with military motifs that immortalized the battle careers of Union officers.

There were scores of irreplaceable gems: General Ulysses S. Grant's death mask and dress uniform and much of what General John F. Reynolds wore when he was killed at the Battle of Gettysburg. A shrine to Abraham Lincoln featured his portraits, a cast of his hands, and documents about his assassination. A room was dedicated to Philadelphia's own General George Gordon Meade, hero of Gettysburg. In a large wooden case in a place of honor hung the most famous relic of all: the mounted head of Meade's favorite horse, Old Baldy, which Civil War veterans dug up from his grave, amputated from his carcass, and carried away on a trolley car.

In a third-floor Victorian parlor stood a rare porcelain doll of Mary Todd Lincoln garbed in her inaugural gown and, on a shelf by the door, a jar of peaches from an orchard on the battlefield of Winchester, Virginia. The elegant lounging jacket of Confederate President Jefferson Davis was among the small cache of Southern items. The jacket was removed from his luggage as a spoil of war on the day he was captured, giving rise to the national scandal that Davis attempted to escape dressed in women's clothing.

Mannequins stood in cases, dressed in officers' coats for a cold day in the campground, so life-like you'd swear you saw their glass eyes blink. The place was filled with ghosts. But the musty aroma that evoked the ghostly spirits actually signaled that the uniforms, flags, letters, and books were moldering away.

The Civil War and Underground Railroad Museum of Philadelphia owns what many believe is the most important stash of Union materials that remain in private hands. For a city like Philadelphia, which makes its bread and butter from heritage tourism, this isn't just another house museum. It's an exceptionally valuable asset because the Civil War is the most popular topic in American history. Every year, Civil War buffs spend millions of dollars on relics, magazines, collectables, classes, tours, and the 50,000 books on the subject. Tens of thousands of reenactors spend their weekends dressed in period garb, fighting long-lost battles on one of the many battlefield sites, while thousands join Civil War heritage organizations and book clubs in places as far away as Australia and Great Britain, and 40 million viewers have tuned in to Ken Burns's series *The Civil War* since it was first aired on public television in 1990. Conflicts rooted in the era—from the propriety of displaying a Confederate flag over South Carolina's capitol to the appropriate restoration of Gettysburg's battlefield—remain front-page news.

Despite the appeal of the Civil War, when I first saw John Brown's pike, its home was in serious trouble. The endowment was depleted, the staff unpaid. Countless letters, diaries, and other documents filled boxes in the musty basement. No one knew how many items there were because no one had ever completely inventoried the collections.

That day, holding John Brown's pike in my hands, I decided to find out why the Civil War Library and Museum remained unvisited, underfunded, and forgotten when so many are so passionate about the Civil War. I wanted to piece together the mystery of how John Brown's pike ended up hundreds of miles away from Harpers Ferry in the basement of this townhouse. And I wanted to save these remarkable treasures.

I began with John Brown. His raid on Harpers Ferry reads like a passage from the Old Testament, and well it should. John Brown was on a mission from God to free the nation from the curse of slavery.

Stephen B. Oates's meticulously researched book *To Purge This Land with Blood* chronicles the life of this controversial abolitionist. Born in Connecticut in 1800, John Brown learned early from his Calvinist parents to revere the Bible and to hate slavery. He married twice and fathered twenty children, struggling to support them through a sad series of bankrupt businesses. But John Brown's achievements as a freedom fighter more than compensated for his lack of acumen as a businessman. From his earliest days, this deeply religious man dedicated his life to the plight of the black slave.

First in Kansas, and later at Harpers Ferry, Brown took his mission to bloody action, fueled by funds from well-heeled and well-intentioned abolitionists, including some Philadelphians, since the city was a hotbed of abolitionist sympathizers. Over the years, Brown fashioned a grand plan: to capture the federal arsenal at Harpers Ferry, located in the Blue Ridge Mountains of Northern Virginia, which manufactured 10,000 guns per year. He would mount a swift and secret attack, secure the town's cache of rifles and ammunition, and use them to launch a major insurrection. Word of his invasion would spread like wildfire. Brown's small contingent of freedom fighters would swell with new recruits, including white sympathizers of the cause and the thousands of free and enslaved blacks from nearby Maryland and Virginia. The rapidly growing band of guerrillas would spill out of Harpers Ferry and down through the South, liberating slaves, confiscating arms and provisions, and spreading its reign of terror.

By 1859, with a substantial war chest in hand, John Brown was ready to transform dream into bloody action. He recruited a small band of conspirators and assembled an arsenal of weapons. Among them was pike number 584, the one owned by the Civil War Library and Museum. It was one of 950 that Brown had purchased from Charles Blair, forge master of the Collins Company, one of the nation's foremost manufacturers of edged tools.

The pikes from the Collins Company were slated to arm the slaves Brown believed would rise up as a result of his victory at Harpers Ferry. While his notion of pitting slaves bearing pikes against soldiers bearing guns may at first appear as a symptom of Brown's considerable delusion, it actually made perfect sense at the time.

Rifles from this period took seven steps to load and fire. "You needed special training, which slaves most certainly would not have," explained a volunteer. "Pikes are more self-evident; you just point and stick."

John Brown arrived in Harpers Ferry in July 1859 and rented a farmhouse nearby to serve as his base of operations. On October 16, 1859, Brown assembled his tiny band of twenty-one recruits—sixteen whites and five blacks—for fervent Sunday prayer. In the chilly and moonless night, he loaded a wagon with instruments of war and led his men "as solemnly as a funeral procession" into Harpers Ferry. Silently, they crossed a bridge, entered the town, and soon captured the sleepy night watchman who was guarding the armory. "I have possession now of the United States armory," Brown told the frightened watchman, "and if the citizens interfere with me I must only burn the town and have blood." By midnight, he had captured a number of hostages and several millions of dollars' worth of federal munitions and arms.

Word of the insurrection was tolled by church bells through the area and carried by an express train that Brown let through to carry the message beyond. Newspapers throughout the East and South blazed the headline: "Negro Insurrection at Harpers Ferry!" In every hamlet and township within a thirty-mile radius, farmers and shop owners grabbed rifles and pitchforks and rushed to Harpers Ferry to repress the rebellion.

By 11 a.m. on October 17, a full battle raged around the arsenal. Brown was stunned by how quickly local militia and farmers came to the call. In the massive confusion, Brown had ample time to take his troops and hostages and make a run for it. Instead, he gathered his men, including armed slaves, and eleven of his most important prisoners and prepared for the inevitable attack.

With rain falling and sporadic fighting continuing, federal troops were arriving by train from Baltimore. Throughout the night of October 17, Brown stood guard in the engine house, watching as the wounded prisoners and fighters lay dying. At first light on the morning of October 18, Brown and his dwindling band looked through the gun holes they had carved in the wall. Instead of the runaway slaves Brown imagined would come, he found a company of the United States Marine Corps led by Brevet Colonel Robert E. Lee. The insurrection had failed. But John Brown was an agent from God, and he would not be daunted.

With 2,000 spectators looking on, Brown refused Colonel Lee's terms for unconditional surrender. Immediately, the troops stormed the engine house, killing raiders, freeing hostages, and wounding Brown in the head. Later that day, a federal patrol captured the farmhouse where the Brown contingent had rested earlier, confiscating all of the remaining pikes and a cache of papers that incriminated Brown and his backers.

John Brown's war for slave liberation lasted only thirty-six hours and cost seventeen lives, including two slaves and two of Brown's own sons. Not a single slave had come to Harpers Ferry on his or her own volition. Brown was quickly brought to trial and convicted of treason against the Commonwealth of Virginia. A fighter to the last, Brown was determined that his message would survive even if he did not. As he walked to the gallows on December 2, Brown passed a note to one of his attendants. It read, in part, "I John Brown am now quite *certain* that the crimes of this *guilty land* will never be purged *away* but with Blood."

These last words proved prophetic. Brown's sensational attack on Harpers Ferry fueled Southerners' greatest fear: a black slave insurrection supported by an invasion from the North. Before Harpers Ferry, the United States was a single nation with a single army. After it, the South began to arm seriously. Within eighteen months of Brown's hanging, seven Southern states had seceded, Colonel Robert E. Lee had declined to fight for the Union and had joined the Confederate cause, and war had begun at Fort Sumter.

Although John Brown's life had ended, the story of his pike was just beginning. In Washington, angry Southern Democratic senators quickly formed a special committee to investigate Northern Republican involvement in Brown's campaign. They interrogated the shocked Charles Blair, manufacturer of John Brown's 950 pikes. When Blair persuaded the senators that he had no knowledge of Brown's plan, they set him free.

At the same time, in Harpers Ferry, another kind of action was taking place. Soon after Brown's raid, its enterprising residents began to sell John Brown's pikes to the thousands of antebellum tourists who flocked to the town. When the locals ran out of authentic pikes, they began to sell fake ones. In one of the ironies of today's exploding market for Civil War memorabilia, these ersatz John Brown pikes now command a higher price than the authentic ones, since the fakes are rarer.

Museum curators learn to study objects closely to determine their provenance, the history of their ownership. The provenance was written all over John Brown's pike, each mark a clue to its mystery. The number 584 stamped on its cross guard and collar was the first clue, verifying that the pike was authentic, not fake, manufactured by the Collins factory. An old paper tag on the pike held the second clue: "McGuire was surgeon on the staff of Stonewall Jackson. Attended him when he was fatally wounded at Chancellorsville."

Dr. Hunter Holmes McGuire was the pike's first post–John Brown owner. Born in 1835 in Winchester, Virginia, he volunteered for the Confederate Army and was soon appointed a surgeon.

McGuire may have secured John Brown's pike in 1861 while he was stationed at Harpers Ferry during the war. Or he might have secured it later from General Stonewall Jackson, who was at the scene during John Brown's raid. As medical director of the second corps, Army of Northern Virginia at Chancellorsville, McGuire attended General Jackson as he lay dying from wounds and pneumonia.

The next clues were painted on the shaft: "Brown's spear from Harpers Ferry presented by Dr. McGuire of Winchester VA 1865 L. Dr. C. H. Meirs, Phila. 1905 By S. F. Meigs Loyal Legion Museum."

In 1865, near the war's end, McGuire apparently met Dr. Meirs from Philadelphia and presented the relic to him. Meirs must have eventually handed the pike over to another Philadelphian, General Montgomery Cunningham Meigs. General Meigs, at the time, was quartermaster general of the U.S. Army.

John Brown's pike number 584 came from manufacturer Collins, who sold it to Brown, who left it at Harpers Ferry, where Dr. McGuire picked it up and later handed it to Dr. Meirs, who passed it along to General Meigs. How did it get to the museum?

On the shaft was a metal plate with the inscription "Presented by Companion S. F. Meigs."

After the war, General Meigs moved to Philadelphia. When he died in 1892, John Brown's pike became the property of his son, S. F. Meigs, who, as a descendant of a Loyal Legion member, is called a companion. In 1905, S. F. Meigs donated it to the War Library and Museum of the Military Order of the Loyal Legion of the United States, the original name of the Civil War Library and Museum.

By this time I knew I was standing in a Civil War shrine as fascinating, or perhaps even more fascinating, than any single item inside it. Its roots reach back to April 15, 1865, the day Lincoln died. Spurred by fear of a larger Southern conspiracy, three Union officers met in Philadelphia's Union League, a private club founded to support the Union cause. No one knew whether Lincoln's assassination was the act of a single zealot or part of a gigantic, secret Southern conspiracy. The officers decided on the spot to form an honor guard to protect Lincoln's body during its solemn route from Washington north through Philadelphia and then on to its final resting place in Springfield, Illinois. Within a year, the Military Order of the Loyal Legion of the United States was founded as a Union officers' honorary society.

Soon the group needed a home, a place where veterans and their families could place their cherished relics for perpetual care. In 1888, Loyal Legion members founded a War Library and Museum as a separate entity, America's first officially chartered Civil War institution. They chose Philadelphia as the site of their national headquarters in honor of its central role in the great conflict.

Few today realize that Philadelphia, then the nation's industrial center, was a major force in the conflict. It was home to Independence Hall and the Liberty Bell, the most potent symbols of the Union, a fact that was not lost on Abraham Lincoln, who visited them on the way to his inauguration. Philadelphia held the largest free black population and was a hub of abolitionist sentiment. Area families, both black and white, hid escaping slaves in stops along the Underground Railroad. African Americans joined the eleven regiments of volunteers who trained at Camp William Penn just over the city's border. Philadelphia was also a place with deep connections to the South through marriage and money. Its factories fueled the war effort; its women held huge fairs to raise funds for critical medical supplies. More Union troops passed through Philadelphia, and more of the sick and wounded were treated there, than in any other city. What was obvious at the time the Loyal Legion was founded drifted slowly into the memory bin of this great city.

By the time that John Brown's pike was donated in 1905, the Loyal Legion boasted a membership of some 8,000 former officers and their direct descendants, including five presidents of the United States. In 1922 the Library and Museum moved to its present Pine Street row house, along with the Loyal Legion's national and Pennsylvania headquarters. That's the "U.S. Commandery-in-Chief" and the "Commandery of the State of Penna" inscribed on the plaque on the façade of the museum.

Unfortunately, time did not smile fondly on this private hereditary society. By the 1940s, its original members and many of their sons were gone; by the 1970s, so was the bulk of the endowment that paid the bills. Spurred by the United States bicentennial celebration in 1976, Loyal Legion members decided to bite the bullet and open their War Library and Museum to the public. Eleven years later, in 1986, the organization's name was changed to the Civil War Library and Museum, and the first non–Loyal Legion members were invited to join the board. The new name and the changes to the bylaws were intended to signal a more public role and pave the way to philanthropic contributions. However, the dollars the board imagined would care for the collection and update the exhibits failed to materialize.

By 2000 the place was broke. There was no money to insure the 3,000 artifacts, 7,000 original photographs, 12,000-volume library, or 400 linear feet of manuscripts, documents, and letters. There was no money to install the kind of environmental or security systems they desperately needed. As a sad consequence, the uniforms worn by the most important Union officers in the most significant battles of America's most wrenching war were slowly self-destructing. The museum owned close to seventy flags that were desperately in need of care, including General Meade's headquarters' flag from Gettysburg. In 1996 an expert estimated that it would cost $250,000 to conserve the flags.

There was no money to pay the staff. The executive director, who had served for four and a half years, and the curator, who had served for eight, resigned. They joined the dedicated but dwindling corps of volunteers who struggled valiantly to keep the place open on a limited basis under the direst of conditions.

There's never only one reason a museum fails to meet its mark. For the Civil War Library and Museum, the reasons include the Loyal Legion's shrinking ranks and the problems private clubs face when they try to go public. There was the institution, which never developed the fund-raising, marketing, and public programming infrastructure that transforms a collection into an operating museum. There was the stuff itself; often the more fragile the object, the more expensive its care. There was the building; it was just too small, too off the beaten track, and, with its steep stairs, too inaccessible to people with mobility problems. And the final reason lay in Philadelphia's fixations on its singular role during the American Revolution and on the U.S. Constitution, which gave the Civil War and other facets of local history short shrift.

Whatever the reasons, the fact remained that these crown jewels of Civil War history deserved more than the loving hands of a committed corps of volunteers. They deserved a new home where the souvenirs and relics would be safe and the public could see and learn from them. The guns and dressing gown, flags and bullet-filled tree stumps, photographs, prints, stuffed horse's head, jar of peach jam, and John Brown's pike—along with relics buried in the vaults of other area institutions—were the ingredients of a sensational Civil War museum.

Happily, this may soon become a reality. After decades of obscurity, the plight of the Civil War Library and Museum finally went public when the board, faced with an all but depleted bank account, decided to move its precious Union relics to the Tredegar National Civil War Center, which was building a new museum in Richmond, Virginia, home of the Confederacy. Philadelphia is a city that takes its heritage very seriously. When word leaked out about the board's decision, a number of locals got very busy.

Spurred by two powerful Philadelphia political leaders, a state senator and a member of the House of Representatives, Pennsylvania's attorney general brought suit in Orphans' Court. The original owners of the collection joined the fray: the Military Order of the Loyal Legion of the United States, Commandery-in-Chief; and the Military Order of the Loyal Legion, Commandery for the State of Pennsylvania. Angered that a precious part of Philadelphia's Civil War heritage was about to retreat south, a coalition of cultural advocates and leaders of cultural institutions crafted a proposal to keep the collection in town. I signed up as member of the Union League, a private club with a sizable Civil War collection of its own.

The heated legal battle that ensued laid bare the crux of the conflict: who owns a museum collection? The board of the Library and Museum argued that as a private institution it had the right to determine its fate. The Tredegar Museum in Richmond promised to become a major, national attraction and thus the most fitting place for the Library and Museum's cherished relics. There was even some discussion of a plan to create a satellite of the Tredegar in Philadelphia and to circulate some of the relics from South to North. The attorney general and other parties in the suit argued that a museum's collection is not the sole province of its board; it's a civic asset, an essential part of the local historic fabric. Newspaper coverage woke area residents to the extraordinary legacy they were about to lose.

When it comes to the Civil War, tempers flare; nothing is ever easy. In Philadelphia, more than 140 years after General Robert E. Lee surrendered to General Ulysses S. Grant at Appomattox, the fighting continued, this time in the courtroom and the press. In late 2002, the parties finally negotiated a settlement. The Commonwealth of Pennsylvania promised to match up to $15 million to build a new Civil War museum for Philadelphia, but only if the board of the Civil War Library and Museum would relinquish control. A new board, comprising representatives of the Civil War Library and Museum, the Military Order of the Loyal Legion, and the public at large, would oversee the collection. The new board would create a new museum to give Philadelphia's Civil War heritage its rightful due.

The settlement agreement also opened the possibility for many of the documents and books to move to a new special collections library open to the public at the Union League of Philadelphia, the place where the story of the Military Order of the Loyal Legion began. Until then, the Civil War Library and Museum, with Brown's pike and all the other treasures, would remain open.

All of this got some of us thinking about Philadelphia's long-hidden Civil War heritage. We knew that countless remnants of this legacy remained. Diaries and dresses, swords and sabers, photographs, paintings, posters, prints, and tons of documents were buried deep in basement storage crypts and up in attic storerooms of regional museums, libraries, and historical societies. Civil War buildings, statues, and monuments dotted the landscape. I was among the Union League members who invited directors of institutions with Civil War holdings—including the Civil War Library and Museum and Grand Army of the Republic Civil War Museum—to explore interest in excavating Philadelphia's long-lost Civil War past. Out of this came a region-wide collaborative, the Civil War History Consortium, Inc. Within a few years, over twenty organizations had joined the consortium, Civil War materials had been unearthed in twenty-five institutions, and more than $200,000 in grants had been secured to begin to bring this heritage to light.

The next step was to reinvigorate the Civil War Library and Museum. The newly appointed board, led by attorney E. Harris Baum, once again changed the name. The one they chose, the Civil War and Underground Railroad Museum of Philadelphia, signified a mission expanded to embrace the African American and abolitionist stories. I was hired to help launch the rebirth of this old institution, in line with the court settlement. The first order of business was to assure the safety of the building and collection, a process begun when the William Penn Foundation awarded a generous grant for a team of experts to inventory the collection and assess its condition.

Piece by piece, the experts matched the written records with objects, photographs, documents, and books. Among the most surprising finds were several books and documents related to slavery, the antislavery movement, and the role of African Americans in the Civil War, including slave purchase receipts, copies of William Lloyd Garrison's *The Liberator*, the leading abolitionist newspaper of its time, and a rare first edition of William Still's *The Underground Railroad*, published in 1872.

By the end of 2004, a new professional staff was in place who installed an exhibit on the Underground Railroad and broader antislavery story. John Brown's pike was finally out of the basement and on public display. Over the next two years, planning began on a new home for the museum, slated for the First Bank of the United States in Independence National Historical Park. This was an especially fitting location because the Civil War was the arena in which many of the unresolved issues of the Revolution and U.S. Constitution were played out.

"We plan to continue the story of the quest for independence, to focus on the connections between the national and local stories: the effects of the war on Philadelphia and its people," Baum told me when I came by for an update. "As you know, the collection is primarily materials from Union officers and their descendants, but many of the items have local connections. Many of the officers lived here; their diaries, letters, and battle flags relate not only to the war overall, but to this city.

Moreover, much of the history of the war is here in Philadelphia: it was the economic engine, close to the Mason Dixon line."

"Lee's intention was to invade Philadelphia after winning the battle of Gettysburg. In fact, some locals said they could hear cannon fire from Gettysburg during the terrible battle. We plan to integrate our holdings—hopefully with materials from other institutions—in the stories the museum will tell about the causes of the Civil War, the slavery issue, the heroes and villains, and the role Philadelphia played."

Something a Civil War aficionado said stayed with me during the years I pieced together the mystery of John Brown's pike and its townhouse home, and worked to save them for Philadelphia: "The whole Civil War phenomenon is in many respects unexplainable," he said. "It's almost reached a cult status. People become emotionally magnetized by this terrible event."

Some people debate long-settled arguments over states' rights, some reenact the long-ago battles of Gettysburg, Vicksburg, and Shiloh, while others devote their energies to saving a Civil War treasure trove to create a new museum. The Civil War was a defining moment in American history, when our Constitution and our people were put to the test. It lives on because the issues it raises will never be resolved, the valor it inspired will never die.

SUMMER GARMENTS
OF A TIBETAN
PRINCESS

Tibetan Woman's Hat
Courtesy of the Burke Museum of Natural History and Culture, Catalog Number 80.0/124

SUMMER GARMENTS OF A TIBETAN PRINCESS

Burke Museum of Natural History and Culture

Seven elegant garments lay on a museum laboratory table, each a piece of a lost world. Worn by a Lady Jamyang Sakya, a Tibetan princess and wife of a white-robed lama, they came along on her family's perilous escape over wind-swept wastelands, up frozen mountains and down treacherous cliffs, with the communist Chinese in hot pursuit. These exotic garments spoke to a culture tragically threatened but also alive in a setting remarkably distant from its country of origin. They also revealed what's special about the Burke Museum of Natural History and Culture, the place where the clothes reside.

Set on a knoll on the campus of the University of Washington in Seattle, the Burke is not like its counterparts I know in the East. Its mission stretches well beyond preserving cultural artifacts to helping living communities sustain their culture. The doors of the Burke swing both ways; it invites diverse ethnic communities in and takes its expertise out to them, sharing ownership in the very process of museum making. This activist stance infuses the place with a vitality that often goes missing in more hide-bound institutions.

James Nason, who had recently achieved emeritus status at both the University of Washington and the Burke, first told me about the Tibetan summer garments. "It's not just how these objects are made; it's what they mean that's important," he said. Because I knew so little about Tibet beyond the myth of Shangri-la, I began by searching for the meaning of the princess's clothing in the culture from which they came.

Surrounded on three sides by the world's highest mountains, Tibet is a high plateau the size of western Europe set in the center of Asia. Until the early twentieth century, few Europeans ever visited the place. It remained a mystery—by design—for Tibetans cherished the isolation that preserved their feudal society. Buddhism ran deep in traditional Tibet, its shrines of *mani* stones inscribed with invocations, reliquaries of Buddhist saints, and monasteries visited by constant streams of pilgrims. Over one-quarter of the male population was monks who spent their lives in monasteries pursuing enlightenment through ritual, study, and meditation.

Two parallel hierarchies, one secular, the other religious, ruled the nation, ensuring that political decisions were infused with the spirituality that lay at the heart of society. At the top of this feudal society was the Dalai Lama. Practitioners of Tibetan Buddhism believe that each of the fourteen consecutive Dalai Lamas is the same Dalai Lama, a reincarnation of the first Dalai Lama who ruled Tibet long ago. Below him were other lamas—spiritual teachers and guides—as many as 4,000 at any one time. Some, like the Dalai Lama, are recognized as rebirths of former lamas. Some received this august designation through their spiritual development in this life. Finally, in some very special families, all members with blood relations to the father are considered lamas: males and females.

Jigdal Sakya came from one of these special families, the Sakya-Khon. His full name is His Holiness Jigdal Dagchen Sakya, which takes a bit of cultural linguistics to unravel. The formal title "His Holiness" indicates his high position in the Tibetan community. Dagchen means "lineage holder," a title he inherited from his father and his fathers before him, back twenty-six generations. His followers call him Rinpoche, "the precious one." James Nason, who knows him from their days at the Burke, calls him by his first name, Jigdal.

Names in traditional Tibet can be very confusing because a single one, Sakya, for example, can refer to a number of things. Sakya is the name of one of the four orders of Tibetan Buddhism, which has monasteries throughout Tibet, Bhutan, and India. Sakya is also the name of the city where the order originated, as well as the name of the leading family of both the city of Sakya and the Sakya Buddhist Order, Jigdal's family, whose full name is Sakya-Khon.

The Sakya-Khon lineage is not only long but also distinguished: it is said that the family descended from celestial beings from the realm of heavenly clear light. The Sakya-Khons served as spiritual advisors to the great Mongol conqueror Kublai Khan, ruled much of Central Asia for many years, and spawned many important religious leaders. Jigdal's father, who carried the title of Trichen, which means "holder of the throne," was Tibet's third most important secular ruler. He was also spiritual leader of the Sakya Order. Following tradition, Jigdal's sisters were raised as nuns, his brothers as monks, and all are lamas. Unlike the red-robed monks who remain celibate, Jigdal is a white-robed, married lama, responsible for continuing the family line.

When Jigdal was twenty years old, he met the love of his life, a Sakya Buddhist teenage girl who was on pilgrimage with her family, visiting important monasteries and shrines. Born in a village of thirty-five families in northeastern Tibet, she was named Sonam Tshe Dzom, which means "the uniting of good deeds into a long life," by her uncle, Dezhung Rinpoche, an important lama and titular head of the family. Sonam's father was a Chinese-born Tibetan and a high official in the Chinese government. When she was five, her father was sent to a new post in China and left her life forever.

An only child, Sonam was raised in the company of adults and received a level of academic education rare among girls. Beginning at age eight, she studied literature and religion as the only female student in the class at the nearby Thalang Monastery, where Dezhung Rinpoche lived and taught. When her formal schooling ended at age twelve, another uncle continued her academic studies. At the same time, she learned women's skills: directing the servants, sewing, knitting, cooking, milking yaks, and churning their milk into butter. Tibetan women were the equals of men in many spheres: they joined men in discussions about commercial and family matters. In fact, women held supreme authority over the household.

Sonam's family was the wealthiest in the village. They owned a two-story house with a small herd of farm animals on the first floor and a shrine room on the second, filled with yak butter lamps, brass bowls, religious books, and *thangkas*. These are elaborate picture panels surrounded by textiles that are used as records of and guides for contemplative experience. I like to think Sonam's indomitable spirit, which sustained her through many trials ahead, was a product of her early upbringing.

Sonam's story is chronicled in *Princess in the Land of Snows: The Life of Jamyang Sakya in Tibet.* Co-authored by Jamyang Sakya, Sonam's married name, and Julie Emery, a reporter for the *Seattle Times*, the autobiography brings alive the rich texture of traditional life, which seems all the more exotic because it is gone. The book was published in 1990, thirty years after the family escaped from Tibet. But all that came later.

In 1948, when Sonam's family began its long pilgrimage to Sakya, Tibet had few paved roads or motorized vehicles, so they traveled by horseback and foot, along with other pilgrims, teams of servants, and 300 yaks. Eighteen months later, the group reached the city of Sakya. This great religious center of several thousand residents boasted gold-roofed monasteries, the largest temple in Tibet, and the palaces of two great families. The Phunstok Palace was home to the Sakya-Khon; the Drolma Palace was home to the other noble family.

Because of her uncle's august stature, Sonam's family was offered rooms in the Sakya-Khon's summer palace, which stood on the grounds of their main palace, the Phuntsok Palace. Two of the Trichen's young daughters befriended her and included her in family games and outings. Jigdal, their oldest brother and heir apparent to the Trichen title, was on the lookout for a wife. When he saw the lovely Sonam, he decided she was the one to bear his children and continue the family line.

While American teenage girls were mooning over Frank Sinatra, going on dates to the movies, and stealing kisses on the front stoop, their Tibetan counterparts were performing intricate group dances, playing games with yak knuckles, and touching foreheads. But courtship is courtship, whatever the culture. The one between Tibetan royalty and the girl from the tiny village featured all of the trappings of high romance. Secret notes passed by a trusted household servant. Clandestine rendezvous in dark stairways. Furtive exchanges of valued gifts. Jigdal's mother objected to Sonam's commoner lineage, wanting her son to marry into a noble family. Sonam and her mother knew he was above her, and moreover, she would have to relinquish her life in her beloved village.

With the guidance of the Sakya-Khon family oracle, a couple of for-tuitous omens, and an especially propitious dream featuring five yellow roses, the lovers eventually overcame all objections. They were married in the Gold Room of Phuntsok Palace. In the ancient ceremony that in-cluded monks, saffron, bells, butter, and prayer beads, the Trichen handed Sonam a white paper wrapped in a scarf. On it was her official name, the one she would use from then on in official correspondence. Sonam Tshe Dzom became Jamyang Pema Palgyiburtri, meaning "the deity of wisdom, the lotus who brings forth many sons." Twenty-four rooms of the summer palace where Sonam's family had stayed became the new couple's honeymoon home.

Sonam's—now Lady Jamyang's—new mother-in-law set out to train her new daughter in the ways of nobility, and there was a lot of train-ing to do, for the wife of an important lama was filled with many re-sponsibilities. For one thing, Lady Jamyang had to learn to balance her new special-occasion headdress, a memorable item in the shape of an archery bow that rose over her head and extended a foot beyond each ear. Lavishly decorated with coral, turquoise, pearls, and rubies, it weighed in at twenty-five pounds, so heavy it made her neck ache. Lady Jamyang also had to learn how to preside over religious festivals and to become accustomed to the crowds that cheered every time the noble family left home.

Within a year the Trichen died and Jigdal inherited the title. But not for long. Through a political sleight of hand, the nobles of the Drolma Palace had secured the Dalai Lama's blessing and within eight months took over the title of Trichen, which by all rights belonged to Jigdal.

This seemed an auspicious time for Jigdal to take his young family across Tibet to visit monasteries and Lady Jamyang's childhood home. Lady Jamyang's memoir took on a darker hue as she described how her family experienced firsthand China's devastating invasion of Tibet. Since the 1700s, China had held titular jurisdiction over Tibet's 7 mil-lion people, allowing their leaders to reign over political and religious matters. But on New Year's Day 1950, three months after the founding of the People's Republic of China, Peking announced its intentions to "liberate" Tibet. The communists promised a gentle modernization that would preserve Tibet's religious ways but that in fact carried the seeds of its destruction.

Jigdal and his family's journey began with the traditional trappings. There were lavish tents, many monks and retainers, and yaks bearing gifts: money, jewels, white scarves, blocks of tea, and the ubiquitous yak butter. Yak butter plays an especially important role in Tibetan life: drunk in tea, given as gifts, and constructed by monks into *tormas*, large, multicolored sculptures of Buddhist figures, for many annual celebrations, including the great Butter Festival. In fact, the Burke Museum owns two plastic pouches of yak butter, hardened into cubes and knotted on ropes made of cotton and yak hair.

As the royal retinue slowly traversed the landscape, signs of the new regime appeared, at first subtle, then overt. New barracks that housed communist troops. New schools where Tibetan children learned the party line. Loudspeakers that blared propaganda through the ancient streets of ancient cities. Soon the monasteries were under attack, their monks kidnapped and forced to wear Chinese soldier's uniforms to fill the front lines of battle.

Imbued with the peaceful ways of Buddhism, isolated from the rest of the world, with an army of fewer than 9,000 soldiers, the Tibetans were ill equipped to resist. Some fled to the hills to join small bands of guerrilla fighters; others acquiesced and were paid well by the Chinese for their support. Those of noble lineage like the Sakya-Khons represented a special target, for their endorsement of the communists would inevitably sway their countrymen.

In the fall of 1954, Jigdal joined the Dalai Lama and other Tibetan dignitaries on a mission to China to try to persuade Mao Tse-tung to honor his promise to protect religious customs and institutions. Their failure spoke to the hopelessness of the Tibetan cause.

When, after four and a half years, Jigdal's retinue returned home, Sakya was overrun with Chinese. To make matters worse, the Drolma and Phuntsok palaces were disputing a debt as well as the Trichen title. Jigdal decided to bring his side of the dispute before the Dalai Lama, so he, his wife, two small children, and retainers set out again, this time for Lhasa, the capital of Tibet. They never saw their home again.

Lhasa was a city transformed into a caldron of intrigue and fruitless resistance to an overwhelming force. In early 1959, the Dalai Lama fled Lhasa. A few days later, Jigdal and Lady Jamyang, their three sons—one an infant—the elderly monk Dezhung Rinpoche, and a small retinue sneaked out of town. When the group split to avoid detection, Lady Jamyang's peace-loving husband handed her a pistol and eleven bullets to use in case of emergency. When they learned that Lhasa was under attack, the choices were clear: capture by the communists or flight to Bhutan, the path to India and freedom.

Jigdal's family was ill prepared for escape: virtually all its possessions and wealth remained in Sakya. More ominously, the route to Bhutan led over the one of the world's largest mountains, Mona Kachung, almost 25,000 feet high at its summit. They packed up and started off, with the communists hot on their trail. The contingent met bands of patriotic Tibetan guerrillas, armed with swords and long sticks, crossed the Tsangpo River in small yakskin boats, and lived off the land and the generosity of the monks and peasants. A Chinese plane emblazoned with a big red star attacked the party while it crossed open land; the only shelter in sight was a farmhouse, but the owner refused to give them shelter. Without compass or maps, Dezhung Rinpoche employed divination to determine their route.

It took two days to scale Mona Kachung. With little food and none of the accoutrements of modern mountaineers—no sun goggles, parkas, or ropes; no oxygen gear or medicine to ward off altitude sickness—the party used what little it had. Jigdal and the two older boys encased their heads in knitted hoods that exposed only their eyes and mouths. Lady Jamyang tied her baby to her body and covered her head with a long embroidered silk scarf that froze from her breath. They joined the long line of refugees who trekked through snow as deep as four feet and climbed over rocks slippery with ice, their eyes burned by the glare of the sun. Sometimes they rode on horses; other times they pushed the exhausted animals up the mountain. Most discouraging of all was the disheartened refugees returning home, forced back by soldiers from the Bhutanese border.

Near the summit, the group stopped to circumambulate a shrine of *mani* stones and prayer flags. With the wind piercing her face like needles, Lady Jamyang gazed at the awe-inspiring view of the Himalayan range: frozen Tibet to the north, the land of the past; green Bhutan to the south, the land of the future.

Beyond the base of Mona Kachung lay the Bhutanese border. With 1,700 other refugees, these remnants of Tibet's royalty awaited permission to cross. Fearing the Chinese would use the Tibetans' admittance as an excuse to invade, the Bhutanese initially refused. Bhutan's prime minister eventually arrived with a letter from the king allowing all the refugees in. The letter specifically noted the Sakya Phuntsok Palace lamas.

The seven garments in the Burke Museum came from this moment in time. According to the ethnology catalog report, the robe, blouse, jacket, apron, boots, scarf, and hat were made in 1958 and worn by "the wife of Rinpoche Sakya prior to her fleeing Tibet at the time of Chinese takeover in 1958." These "modern summer garments of a woman of high rank" were among the few possessions Lady Jamyang carried on this perilous journey, "dress up" clothes given to her as a gift in Tibet. The Burke had purchased them in 1962, soon after the family's arrival in Seattle.

The long sleeveless robe is a *chuba*, the traditional garb of Tibetan women, which is made of luminous magenta satin brocaded with pink and green flowers and closed by a button under the right arm. The blouse worn under the chuba is the only modern-looking garment, a blue and green flowered rayon print. Around the waist of the *chuba*, Lady Jamyang tied the traditional cotton striped apron of married Tibetan women. This one features sparkling metallic brocade on its upper corners that matches the brocade on her hat: a high-crowned item with four fur flaps to protect her face, neck, and both sides of her head. A lavishly embroidered jacket of teal blue silk and a long pale-pink silk scarf complete the ensemble.

Most striking were Lady Jamyang's black and red wool boots decorated with colorful embroidery and brocade. The backs of the boots were slit from top to calf, likely held to the leg by cloth ties. In her memoir Lady Jamyang describes how, when she was a teenager, a boy showed his affection by slipping a cloth tie off one of her boots.

Crowds greeted the royal refugees as they made their way across Bhutan. They crossed the border to India, eventually ending up in Darjeeling, where a wealthy Sherpa took them in. It was there the family learned that Lady Jamyang's mother and aunt had decided to remain in Sakya to protect the palace and its valuable contents. They later died in a communist Chinese prison.

At the Dalai Lama's request, Jigdal assumed his traditional role as head of the Sakya Order of Tibetan Buddhism and began touring monasteries throughout India. Soon he met two British educators who were in India studying Tibetan culture. They befriended the noble family, offered Jigdal a three-year research position in France, and eventually introduced him to another scholar, Turrell V. Wylie of the University of Washington, who offered another three-year research grant, this one from the Rockefeller Foundation. Using divination, Jigdal decided on the United States, especially since this meant the family could stay together. Since the royals were destitute, Professor Wylie advanced some of the Rockefeller money.

In October 1960, before a crowd of Indians, Tibetan refugees, photographers and news reporters, Professor Wylie, and eight Tibetan nobles—Jigdal, his brother, sister, wife, and three sons, and Lady Jamyang's uncle, Dezhung Rinpoche—boarded a Pan Am plane and flew from Calcutta to Seattle. They were among the first Tibetan refugees to enter the United States. They never believed Seattle would become their permanent home.

Seattle is known for its rain, and the day I first saw Lady Jamyang's summer garments was cold and raw. James Nason greeted me at the employee entrance, unlocked the door to the ethnology department, and led me into the processing laboratory. It was banked with cabinets filled with curatorial files and chests of drawers filled with curatorial tools: pencils and tape measurers, archival plastic bags. A Polynesian *tapa* cloth hung on a wall; a Navajo painting lay near a peculiar wooden sculpture that looked like a hat atop a base carved with palm trees sprouting leaves of chicken feathers.

"This is also where we train students in our graduate museology program," said Nason. "The University of Washington's was one of the first museum programs of its type in the country. Now people from all over the world come to study at the Burke."

The origins of the Burke Museum of Natural History and Culture reach back to the time before Washington attained statehood and much of Seattle was forest and farm. In 1880 a group of young men founded the Young Naturalists society to collect and educate themselves about the flora and fauna of their Northwest home. Within a few years, they had forged a relationship with the new Washington Territorial University, raised funds to construct a museum, and in 1899 secured designation from the new state legislature as the official museum of Washington State.

These Young Naturalists weren't the only ones collecting Northwest materials; a wealthy couple was interested in it too. Thomas Burke was an immigrant Irishman who made his fortune in gold mines and owned the largest pornographic store in Seattle. Also a judge, he was an out-spoken supporter of the rights of Chinese immigrants and Native Americans. "One day a gang of angry Seattleites dragged all of the Chinese immigrants to the docks to drive them out of the country. I've read that Thomas Burke appeared on the scene, shot the ringleader dead, and took care of the Chinese," Nason told me.

Caroline Burke, Thomas's wife, was fascinated by Native Americans and entertained her friends in Indian dress at her lakeside home, which was filled with Indian materials of all kinds. Her large collection of Native American materials came to the museum in 1932, and the family's estate was used to partially underwrite construction of the Thomas Burke Memorial Washington State Museum.

"I first met Jigdal when I was a graduate student at the University of Washington in the 1960s," Nason remembered. "He had recently been brought to Seattle by the United States government and the Rockefeller Foundation to work with our small Tibetan collection. The director of the Burke at the time had an interest in Asian costume. I remember when Jigdal brought his wife, siblings, and uncle to my wedding. It was held in a small church, and when the minister started to speak, the Tibetan monks began to chant their own prayers. At the end of the ceremony, Jigdal and his relatives threw white scarves around my wife's neck and mine, reached up high—he's pretty short—and tapped heads against ours," Nason recalled with a smile.

"Let me show you the masks Jigdal made when he worked here in the 1960s for an exhibit about Tibetan culture." Nason led me to the ethnology department's storage room. Every shelf in the long room was covered with very strange stuff: a Melanesian mask, five feet tall, worn by boys in a sacred ceremony; three pigs woven by the Sepik people of New Guinea; many, many Native American objects, including a number of gorgeous carvings by a contemporary Northwestern artist; a ghost trap created by Jigdal himself, which looks like a four-foot-tall house woven from colored wool. "Ghosts are generally bad things," Nason explained, "though I don't know about Tibet."

We entered a corridor between two banks of compactor shelving where the Tibetan materials are kept. Nason climbed nimbly up a fifteen-foot ladder and reached for an oversized, dark-brown papier-mâché mask of Sbag-ma, a clown, with six human teeth in its red-rimmed mouth, white fur hair, eyebrows, moustache, and a small goatee. "Hmm, let's see what else is up here," he said, looking at a nearby shelf. "Statues of Buddha, bells, whistles, and trumpets made out of shells and a human thighbone."

"Can I take a look?" I asked eagerly.

"Sure," said Nason. He climbed down the ladder and held it while I climbed up. The metal shelves were covered with Ethafoam, a non-reactive, plastic material upon which sat forty-seven papier-mâché masks with ornately painted, cartoon-like faces. Many were of deities with three eyes and crowns of skulls. One particularly memorable deity had a face decorated with gold designs, three eyes encircled with bright pink and outlined in gold, and a wide pink mouth with seventeen teeth, four of them fangs, and two fans of polychrome paper where its ears would have been. Many were animals: a black bull with a smiling face, a brown bear, yak, mouse, and lion. Monks had worn similar masks in the Dance of Twenty-One Creatures, "staged only at Sa-skaa Tibet in 7th month of Tibetan Lunar Year," read the catalog. Lady Jamyang wrote of repairing similar animal masks for Torgyak, the annual festival and ceremonial reading of the more than one hundred volumes of the sacred *Kanj*.

James Nason is a tall and commanding member of the Comanche tribe who speaks in the measured cadence of a university professor. He has had a fascinating career: director of the University of Washington's Graduate Museology Program, professor in its Department of Anthropology, and curator of Pacific and American Ethnology at the Burke. With so many objects under his care, I wondered why he was so drawn to those from Tibet.

"I've always thought that the transfer of Lady Jamyang's objects to the museum was emblematic of the very important transition to American life by this very important Tibetan family," he said. "In my mind it represented their family and country and their pride connected to it. These objects could also represent for us massive change."

"Massive change?" I repeated.

"Yes, everything in our ethnology collection is connected to change. Anthropologists talk about change a lot but don't often see it in connection to a particular person or family at a particular moment. These kinds of transitions are often hard to get at unless you have a personal example."

We walked through the locked storeroom door into the galleries and up a flight of stairs. Near the entrance to the Burke was a case of

Suquamish Indian materials. "The Burke is on Suquamish lands; Chief Seattle was a Suquamish. Whenever we open a new exhibit, a Suquamish leader comes to give the welcome and blessing," he said.

How curious, I thought. Politicians and corporate donors often give speeches at openings, but I had never heard of a tribal member asked to give a blessing. There was clearly something different about the Burke.

We came to an exhibit about the natural history of the Northwest, beginning with the dinosaurs and moving up to today. Across the way, in the gallery used for temporary shows, a series of *thangkas* was hung on walls, across the room from thirty-six exotic photographs of Tibet, China, and Mongolia from the 1920s, on loan from Harvard University.

"We purchased these *thangkas* from a dealer. I believe Jigdal helped with this," said Nason. "At the time, there was quite a bit of Tibetan material on the market. Apparently the Chinese communists had removed it from the temples and monasteries and put it up for sale. Museums in those days had no problem with such purchases so long as the paperwork was good. You had to be absolutely certain about the provenance. Now, most of what we purchase is new, very new."

Very new? The natural history and anthropology museums I knew were interested in the very *old*—dinosaur bones, Egyptian mummies, ancient pots from ancient civilizations and the like—not the very new. I understood the need to preserve traditional materials like Lady Jamyang's summer garments, but why save her husband's masks? Were they more than simply props created in the 1960s for an exhibit?

Nason led me downstairs to *Pacific Voices*, a permanent installation that illustrates the cultures of seventeen Pacific Rim communities represented in Seattle. "One of our goals at the Burke, and it is not usually done in the same way in many museums, is to provide cultural meaning for objects on display," explained Nason. "This exhibit is an example. Beginning in the 1980s, we developed policies to give voice to the community through its direct involvement in planning and executing exhibits. That policy was expanded and refined in the 1990s with *Pacific Voices*, which drew on a very diverse set of communities. Two or three key advisors from each community met together weekly, then monthly, to agree on the major themes. Then, each of the communities selected objects and wrote labels and other copy for its own exhibit. The displays represent who *they* are to the public. Not everyone agreed on every item," he remembered, "and that's fine. We just put the differences on the labels."

"The cases in *Pacific Voices* mix historical and contemporary materials," I said, in surprise, looking at the long case that displayed an array of Native American objects. "Why do you collect contemporary items? Why are they relevant?"

"Because the Burke is all about continuity," he explained. He stopped to think for a moment. "Most museums in this country are small historical societies. Many young people first encounter Native American arrowheads, tomahawks, pottery, and the like during school field trips to these places. If these historical societies portray Native Americans only as people who lived long ago, the students will think their culture is dead. These are living cultures, vitally alive today."

We moved on to an exhibit about the Filipino community, which featured a large statue of the Virgin Mary holding Baby Jesus that sat atop a platform. "This is Santo Nino. People from the community went back to the Philippines to bring it here. See the holes at the base? Every year, members of the community come in, insert long poles in the holes, and carry Santo Nino out for the procession of the Festival of the Holy Child."

"You actually let people take things out of the museum?" I asked in amazement.

"Yes," said Nason. "These objects are very important to them; we know they'll take good care of them. We want our museum to be a place where people from a community can see their things and use them. Here's another example: in the 1960s, along with the masks and ghost catcher, Jigdal oversaw the creation of a large drum for the exhibit about Tibetan culture. When he founded the Sakya Buddhist monastery, he asked for it back and we de-accessioned it to him. You may want to see the monastery; it's close by."

The next day I went to the Sakya Monastery of Tibetan Buddhism, which is located in a former church on a residential street in the Greenwood section of Seattle. The walls and ceilings of its large shrine room are painted with clouds and Buddhist deities and hung with *thangkas* paintings like the ones at the Burke. At the entrance is the drum from the Burke; it is made of sheepskin and wood and held in a large wooden frame. In the center of the elaborately decorated altar is a larger-than-life Buddha, and behind him, a golden cabinet with shelves of statues of deities. Next to the altar is a high platform where His Holiness Jigdal Dagchen Rinpoche sits during religious services. When he's not there in person, his portrait sits in his place.

The monastery is an embodiment of cultural continuity. It serves as the New World center of the Sakya order and continues its traditions in the services where the large drum is beaten during *pujas* for practices like *Mahakala* and *Tso Kor*. A non-denominational learning center, the monastery offers classes, talks, performances, and discussions for anyone interested in Buddhism, Tibetan culture, and religion. The highest-ranking lamas in Tibetan Buddhism, including the Dalai Lama, have visited and consecrated the building.

I spent that evening thinking about Lady Jamyang's traditional garments and Jigdal's contemporary masks, his de-accessioned drum at the Sakya monastery, the mix between old and new objects in the Burke's exhibit cases and storage room, and especially the exquisite care and deep respect afforded to community involvement. I know museums with community outreach programs, ones that stage exhibits and events to appeal to ethnic visitors, and even some that invite ethnic artists to create the occasional show. Never had I seen this degree of intentional, sustained interaction with multiple ethnic communities.

Back at the Burke the next day, I asked James Nason about this.

"Isn't it time consuming to involve the community in exhibition design?" I asked.

"Yes, it is. We need to double the usual amount of time for planning to make sure everyone has his or her say. Connections are very difficult to sustain, for the Burke and for people in the community. But community involvement is really important because our visitors must know that communities aren't frozen, they're living, there's continuity."

These connections have served the museum well, especially in its efforts to fulfill the requirements of the 1990 Native Americans Graves Protection and Repatriation Act. Under this federal law, institutions with Native American holdings must provide summaries and inventories of their objects in five categories: human remains, associated burial goods, unassociated burial goods, sacred objects essential to ongoing religious practice, and objects of cultural patrimony. Tribes then face the arduous process of reviewing the inventories and identifying individual artifacts eligible for return, based on Reparation Act guidelines.

The Burke has 40,000 specimens in its ethnology collection and over a million more in its archeology collection, most of them Native American in origin. To date, it has devoted countless staff hours and over $1 million in working with over thirty tribes in this massive undertaking, and the effort continues.

But the Burke shares more than simply the objects under its care. It also helped create every tribal museum in the Northwest. "We consult, help them find grant money, train their leadership. We even divert collections to their institutions that are offered to the Burke," said Nason proudly.

"What you heard from Jim Nason is nothing new for the Burke," said Julie Stein, director of the Burke. "Since 1899 the Burke has carried a deep commitment to community. It's been part of the ethical fiber, the bricks and mortar of this museum. In the 1970s and 1980s, curators could deny access to the collections. Now, anyone with an interest and patience to wait can see something in the collection, no matter who they are. Remember, the Burke Museum is an agency of state government. We don't own the objects; they're owned by the people of Washington. Our job is to be good stewards."

"So, how do Lady Jamyang's traditional summer garments and Jigdal's contemporary mask and drum connect to the Burke Museum's approach to community?" I asked James Nason.

He thought for a moment. "We want to acquire materials that have meaning to the people they came from. It's not the object; it's what it means. Context. People and events, processes, especially the processes of change. We're interested in how cultures adapt and change."

"I never directly asked Jigdal about it," he continued, "but for me, his and his wife's materials represent the dramatic, poignant shift that took place in the lives of these migrants to America. Think about it. One year Jigdal and his family are in Tibet, actively involved in local custom, and almost in a blink of an eye they're here, in Seattle. Literally everything is different: housing, transportation, and even food. Within a couple of years, one of the sons becomes a high school football star."

Here was the philosophy that lay at the heart of the Burke, I thought. What appeared to be a museum of contradictions was actually a museum of continuity. Just like all of American society, this Seattle-based museum was a place where diverse cultures lived on because they never really died, only changed in response to new circumstances, a new setting.

Although the perilous escape of Tibetan nobles is one of a kind, it is also the story of all American immigrants. Unless we're Native Americans, we own our own heroic stories of fear, flight, and ultimately adjustment to a strange new world. My husband tells this story with a Russian Jewish twist: how his grandparents, mother, uncle, and aunts fled from the pogroms, how it took years to trek across Europe until they reached Belgium, how one of the sons was left behind and another, already in America, paid for their passage across the ocean to Canada and eventually to Buffalo, New York. Today Mexicans, Guatemalans, and Iraqis are living this story, the one they will pass on to their children, their own future high school stars. James Nason says that all of us come from tribes, whether Jewish, Native American, or Tibetan.

Lady Jamyang is now Mrs. Sakya, the mother of five sons, the five yellow roses foretold in her teenage dream. Because of her deep dedication to religious study and practice, she has achieved the designation of lama, like her husband, and the title Dagmola, which means "female teacher." Their story will live on in the hearts of their children and grandchildren and in the masks, the ghost catcher, and the lovely summer garments of this Tibetan princess.

What's next for the Burke? If James Nason's vision comes true, it will become a place with shared trust holdings, where the institution cares for objects that the community owns and uses for religious and other purposes. This is not an impossible dream; New Zealand's Auckland Museum and Maoris have shared trust holdings for fifty years, and a few other museums also follow this policy. Perhaps in the future more far-sighted museums will reach to this higher societal call, sharing the very ownership of their stuff with communities outside their doors.

EPILOGUE

I began this journey through a selection of collecting institutions to search for the behind-the-scenes lessons that all of them hold. I uncovered four of them.

The first lesson is that every collecting institution is itself an artifact with a singular story to tell. Each museum, special collections library, historical society, and archive is born at a specific moment in time, reacts to specific challenges and opportunities, deals with its collections, and connects with its communities in different, often idiosyncratic ways. All follow an evolutionary path that mirrors the path of society. Earnest amateurs founded most museums. Over time, in response to society's evolving needs and values, these institutions morphed into an international mega-cultural industry where public entertainment is almost as important as public education, and where armies of professionals now stand in the places where a few amateurs once stood.

How collecting institutions respond to the ever changing American landscape leads to the second lesson, which confirmed my own experience as director of the Atwater Kent. These places are very tough to manage and even tougher to change. They move at a pace that appears glacial to those in the private sector, but for good reason. It's very tricky to balance competing missions, and trickier still to start something new when there are so few dollars and thus so little room for error. Every day in a museum director's life brings another wrenching choice, for there's never enough money to simultaneously satisfy every priority, to do everything right.

The third lesson gets to these priorities. What's most important: exhibits or collections? When I directed the Atwater Kent Museum, the answer seemed obvious: public exhibits had to come first, since unless the public came, the mayor of Philadelphia would close our doors. What I later realized, quite to my surprise, was something different. If you believe in the intrinsic, civic value of collecting institutions, there's really no choice. Collections must come first—the bones and birds, diaries and documents, creations of master and minor artists, relics, charms, talismans, souvenirs, specimens, and heirlooms. This stuff is the stuff of the scholarship, science, and exhibitions of the future. Preserving it for posterity is the most important thing collecting institutions do.

Whether it's the family portrait hanging in your parlor or the extinct species lying in a drawer in a museum's storage cabinet, the objects we save are touchstones; they tell us who we are. Objects bring forward our personal memories and bind them to the larger story of society. By saving the stuff lost in the museum, we allow future scholars, curators, and visitors to explore themselves in relation to their material heritage. Each succeeding generation brings its own questions and fresh perspectives. Marginal artists are rediscovered and celebrated; specimens are reexamined and new species emerge; segments of society once hidden from view are revealed and celebrated. Years ago, no one would have imagined that today's historians would search archives for clues to the roles that gays and lesbians played in society. But they do. And they couldn't unless past archivists saved the documents.

There are way too many treasures buried in the crypts, but they do not have to remain hidden. Many institutions are finding imaginative ways to bring more of their stuff to public view. The most exciting one is the Internet. Places like the Athenaeum of Philadelphia and the Mütter Museum of the College of Physicians of Philadelphia are digitally documenting their holdings and making them accessible to all via their websites, as will the Barnes Foundation soon. The Carnegie Museums of Pittsburgh and many others are staging temporary exhibitions that bring fresh interpretation to long-lost treasures. Some are offering behind-the-scenes tours. Others are building open storage areas, shelves lined with objects behind walls of glass, so visitors can walk by and view them *in situ*.

These efforts are critically important. There's no other way to convince the public to invest in preservation of the 630 million items that Heritage Preservation and the Institute of Museum and Library Services found in need of immediate care. Studies like these help collecting institutions reveal their massive hidden holdings and justify the costs of preserving them. People don't give to causes they can't see.

Which brings me to the final lesson I learned, and it was the most surprising. Every collecting institution, regardless of size, type, age, or collecting practice, is a storehouse of stories just waiting to be told. And while museum professionals are delighted to show off their favorite treasures, they can lose perspective on what the public would most enjoy. That's where museum visitors can help by sharing their preferences, interests, and perspectives on the stories that resonate most. The Burke Museum of Natural History and Culture is a stunning example of the exhilaration that emerges when the very process of museum making is a collaboration between professionals and community members. Unlock the doors and share the stuff.

My journey of discovery began at the Atwater Kent Museum, so it's fitting that it ends there too. The metal toy train that curator Jeffrey Ray showed me during my first week on the job is still there, along with the 80,000 other objects. In fact, there are more, because the collection now includes the art and artifacts of the Historical Society of Pennsylvania. Under the management of a thoughtful and seasoned executive director, all are now safe, secure, and preserved for our children and our children's children.

The skull of a prehistoric Peruvian child, Audubon's stuffed Carolina parakeets, Thomas Ustick Walter's rendering of the dome of the United States Capitol, even the Mütter Museum's pessaries are essential pieces of our past. Collecting institutions are their stewards, but the stuff belongs to all of us. It's our legacy, the soul of our society.

RESOURCES

For Those Who Want to Learn More

INTRODUCTION: "THE STUFF"

Atwater Kent Museum of Philadelphia
15 South 7th Street
Philadelphia, PA 19106
Phone: 215-685-4830
www.info@philadelphiahistory.org

CHAPTER 1: JOHN JAMES AUDUBON'S BIRDS

Academy of Natural Sciences
1900 Benjamin Franklin Parkway
Philadelphia, PA 19103
Phone: 215-299-1000
www.ansp.org

Irmscher, Christopher, ed. *John James Audubon: Writings and Drawings.*
   New York: Literary Classics of the United States, 1999.
Streshinsky, Shirley. *Audubon: Life and Art in the American Wilderness.*
   New York: Villard Books, 1993.

CHAPTER 2: BLASCHKA SEA ANIMALS

Carnegie Museums of Pittsburgh
4400 Forbes Avenue
Pittsburgh, PA 15213
Phone: 412-622-3131
www.carnegiemuseums.org

Carnegie, Andrew. *Autobiography of Andrew Carnegie*. New York: Houghton Mifflin, 1920.
Lippincott, Louise, and Andreas Bluhm. *Fierce Friends: Artists and Animals, 1750–1900*. London: Merrell, 2005.

CHAPTER 3: FRANKLIN B. GOWEN'S BOWL

Historical Society of Pennsylvania
1300 Locust Street
Philadelphia, PA 19107
Phone: 215-732-6200
www.hsp.org/

Griffith, Sally F. *Serving History in a Changing World: The Historical Society of Pennsylvania in the Twentieth Century*. Philadelphia: Historical Society of Pennsylvania, 2001.
Schlegel, Marvin W. *Ruler of the Reading: The Life of Franklin B. Gowen, 1836–1889*. Harrisburg, PA: Archives Publication Company of Pennsylvania, 1947.

CHAPTER 4: PESSARIES

Mütter Museum of the College of Physicians of Philadelphia
19 South 22nd Street
Philadelphia, PA 19103
Phone: 215-563-3737
www.collphyphil.org/mutter.asp

Worden, Gretchen. *Mütter Museum of the College of Physicians of Philadelphia*. New York: Blast Books, 2002.

CHAPTER 5: SKULL OF A PREHISTORIC PERUVIAN CHILD

Smithsonian Institution, National Museum of Natural History
10th Street and Constitution Avenue, NW
Washington, DC 20560
Phone: 202-633-1000
www.mnh.si.edu

Ortner, Donald. *Identification of Pathological Conditions in Human Skeletal Remains*. New York: Academic Press, 2003.
Ortner, Donald, Erin H. Kimmerle, and Melanie Dietz. "Probable Evidence of Scurvy in Subadults from Archaeological Sites in Peru." *American Journal of Physical Anthropology* 108 (1999): 321–331.

CHAPTER 6: KER-FEAL

Barnes Foundation
300 North Latch's Lane
Merion, PA 19066
Phone: 610-667-0290
www.barnesfoundation.org

Hart, Henry. *Dr. Barnes of Merion*. New York: Farrar, Straus and Giroux, 1963.
Lukacs, John A. *Philadelphia Patricians and Philistines, 1900–1950*. New York: Farrar, Straus and Giroux, 1980.

CHAPTER 7: PLAN FOR THE DOME OF THE UNITED STATES CAPITOL

Athenaeum of Philadelphia
219 South 6th Street
Philadelphia, PA 19106
Phone: 215-925-2688
www.philaathenaeum.org

Moss, Roger W. *Philadelphia Victorian: The Building of the Athenaeum*. Philadelphia: Athenaeum of Philadelphia, 1998.

CHAPTER 8: JOHN BROWN'S PIKE

Civil War and Underground Railroad Museum of Philadelphia
1805 Pine Street
Philadelphia, PA 19103
Phone: 215-735-8196
www.civilwarmuseumphiladelphia.org

Oates, Stephen B. *To Purge This Land with Blood: A Biography of John Brown.* 2nd ed. Amherst: University of Massachusetts Press, 1984.
Weigley, Russell F. *Philadelphia: A Three Hundred Year History.* Philadelphia: Barra Foundation, 1982.

CHAPTER 9: SUMMER GARMENTS OF A TIBETAN PRINCESS

Burke Museum of Natural History and Culture
17th Avenue NE and NE 45th Street
Seattle, WA 98195
Phone: 206-543-5590
www.washington.edu/burkemuseum

Sakya, Jamyang, and Julie Emery. *Princess in the Land of Snows: The Life of Jamyang Sakya in Tibet.* Boston: Shambhala, 2001.

INDEX

Academy of Natural Sciences, 9–22;
    collection of, 13; contact
    information for, 155; mission of,
    21
accession number, 2
activism, museums and, 135
African Americans: Barnes and, 88,
    93; and Civil War, 126, 130
American Institute of Architects,
    111–12
American Museum of Natural
    History, 18
Andy Warhol Museum, 38
anemia, 77
animals, in art, 29, 31–33
anthropology, physical, 77–79
anthropometrics, 78–79
The Apotheosis of George Washington,
    110–11
apron, 142
Archaeotherium mortoni, 28
architecture: Athenaeum collection
    on, 113, 115; Carnegie Museums
    and, 27–28
archives, historical, 101–15
archivists, 49

Argyrol, 89
art museums, 35–37
Ashberry, Mary, 66
Athenaeum of Philadelphia, 101–15;
    building of, 111–12; contact
    information for, 157; website of,
    115, 152
Atwater Kent Museum, 1–8, 153;
    challenges to, 3–4; contact
    information for, 155; and exhibits,
    152; and Historical Society of
    Pennsylvania, 50–51, 54–55;
    stakeholders of, 5
Audubon, John James, 29;
    background of, 14–15; birds of,
    9–22, 9f; fieldwork by, 16–17
Audubon, Lucy Bakewell, 14–15, 17

Bab-edh-Dhra, 82
Bakewell, Lucy, 14–15, 17
Barnes, Albert Coombes, 87–89, 91,
    93
Barnes, Laura, 88, 90–93, 98
Barnes Arboretum School, 92, 98
Barnes Foundation, 85–100; contact
    information for, 152, 157

Baum, E. Harris, 130–31
Becker, Isabel, 110, 112–13
Bhutan, 141–42
Biddle, Nicholas, 106, 115
biological anthropology, 77–79
Birds of America (Audubon), 9–22, 9*f*
Blair, Charles, 122–24
Blaschka, Leopold and Rudolf:
  background of, 30–31; glass sea
  animals by, 23–38, 23*f*
Blühm, Andreas, 33–34
board, 6, 21–22; and de-accessioning,
  128–29; and exhibits, 33; and
  reorganization, 50, 52
Bolivar, 12
boots, 142
Bouvier, Michel, 115
bowl, of Franklin B. Gowen, 39–55,
  39*f*
Brown, John: background of, 122–23;
  pike of, 117–31, 117*f*
Brumidi, Constantino, 110–11
Buckley, Barbara, 96–97
Burke, Caroline, 144
Burke, Thomas, 143–44
Burke Museum of Natural History
  and Culture, 133–50, 133*f*; contact
  information for, 158; founding of,
  143
Burns, Ken, 121
Burr, Aaron, 3
business practice, 49

Camp, Kimberly, 87, 91, 94, 96
Carnegie, Andrew, 26, 28, 36–37
Carnegie Institute, 1–2, 25–26
Carnegie Mellon University, 28
Carnegie Museums of Pittsburgh,
  23–38, 152; contact information
  for, 156
Carolina parakeet, 9*f*, 11, 17–18
cast iron, 107–8

catalogs, 97, 142, 145; electronic, 100;
  of exhibit, 33–34
cervical cap, 63
Chang and Eng, 65
chuba, 142
citrus fruits, 76
Civil War: Philadelphia and, 120, 126,
  128–31; popularity of, 121; Walter
  and, 108
Civil War History Consortium, Inc.,
  130
Civil War and Underground Railroad
  Museum of Philadelphia, 117–31,
  117*f*; contact information for, 158
Clark, William, 12, 21
Cleveland, Grover, 59
climate control. *See* environmental
  conditions
coal, Bowen and, 42–43
collecting institutions: as artifact,
  151; behind the scenes, 3–4,
  151–53; crisis of, 6–7; failure of,
  127–28; focus of, 113; missions of,
  4, 21, 48; of Philadelphia, 7,
  113–14; reform of, 47–55;
  resources on, 155–58; visitors and,
  153
collections, 1–8, 151–53; de-
  accessioning, 48–50; diversity in,
  Worden on, 66; versus exhibits,
  152; ownership of, 128–29;
  rationale for, 20
collections management, 49; at
  Barnes, 94; costs of, 3, 54;
  strategies for, 12–13
College of Physicians of Philadelphia,
  Mütter Museum, 57–68, 57*f*, 152,
  156
Collins Company, 123
community involvement, 146–50
computed tomography, 82
Conan Doyle, Arthur, 44

Congress: and capitol dome, 110–11; and Smithsonian, 81
conjoined twins, 65
conservators, 49, 96–97
Constitution, 42
contemporary items, 147
Conuropsis ludovicianus, 9f, 11, 17–18
Copepoda, 32
Copley, John Singleton, 51
Cousteau, Jacques, 34
Crazy Horse, Roy, 52
CT scanner, 82
curators, 29, 49, 59–62, 64, 99, 127; gloves, 75; and natural history, 35; role of, 66
Curie, Pierre, 61

Dalai Lama, 136, 139–40
Davis, Jefferson, 121
de-accessioning, 45–46, 48–53, 147
de Castro, R., 62
Declaration of Independence, 42
de Mazia, Violette, 92–93
Design Museum, 36
Dewey, John, 88–89
Dezhung Rinpoche, 137, 140–41, 143
Dicles of Carystol, 62
digital inventory, 76–77; of Athenaeum, 115; on Internet, 152
dinosaurs, 21–22, 28
dioramas, 18
directors, 87, 151; challenges of, 7; of education, 46; and financial issues, 13; of professional development, 94–95; qualifications of, 4. *See also* executive directors
disease, in prehistoric specimens, 69–84, 69f
diversity, in collections, Worden on, 66
DNA, 20

dome of the United States capitol, plan for, 101–15, 101f
donors, 50
Drolma Palace, 138–40
drum, Tibetan, 147
Dubuffet, Jean, 29
du Pont, Henry Francis, 92
Dzom, Sonam Tshe. *See* Sakya, Jamyang

Edison, Thomas Alva, 1
education: Carnegie on, 27; director of, 46
educators, 49
Elizabeth II, queen of Great Britain, 37
Emancipation Proclamation, 42
Emerson iron lung, 61, 66
Emery, Julie, 138
endowments, 64; Barnes and, 91, 94; of Civil War Museum, 121
Ennis, Robert, 109–10, 112, 114–15
environmental conditions, 3, 54, 104, 112, 127
ethnic communities, museums and, 135, 147–50
ethnology, 143, 145, 149
eugenics, 78
evolution, 35
executive directors, 2–3, 127, 130, 153. *See also* directors
exhibits, 5; on Audubon, 14, 18–19; versus collections, 152; costs of, 82; *Fierce Friends,* 29, 32, 35, 37; *Finding Philadelphia's Past,* 46; *Origins,* 81–82; *Pacific Voices,* 146–47; philosophy of, 37; planning, 32–38

Fidèle, 88, 91, 93
Fierce Friends, 29, 32, 35, 37
Filipino community, 147

financial issues, 4–6; at Barnes, 95;
    Civil War Museum and, 127; and
    exhibits, 33; mechanisms of, 13;
    Moss on, 113; and reorganization,
    48, 51; Smithsonian and, 81; Stitt
    and, 47
First Bank of the United States, 130
focus, importance of, 113
Forrest, Edwin, 51
Franklin, Benjamin, 42
Franklin Institute, 106
Freedom Theatre, 51
The Free Exchange, 29
freezers: for artifacts, 98; for
    specimens, 20
fund raising, 5–6; Athenaeum and,
    112; Barnes and, 91, 95; for
    exhibits, 33

garments, of Tibetan princess,
    133–50, 133*f*
Garrison, William Lloyd, 130
Gehrung anteversion pessary, 61
genital prolapse, 60, 63
Getty Foundation, 95
Gillman, Derek, 99
Girard, Stephen, 106
Girard College, 104, 106–7, 109–10
Glackens, William J., 89
Glanton, Richard H., 93–94
Global History of Health Project, 84
global warming, 20
gloves, curator's, 75
Gospel of Wealth (Carnegie), 26–27
Gould, John, 19–20
Gowen, Franklin B.: background of,
    42–43; bowl of, 39–55, 39*f*;
    decline of career of, 45
Grant, Ulysses S., 120
Griffith, Sally, 47
gynecology: artifacts of, 57–68, 57*f*;
    practices in, 63

Haeckel, Ernst, 31
Harding, Deborah, 34–35
Harpers Ferry, VA, 119–20, 122–24
Harris, Edward, 17
Harry Winston Gallery, 81
Harvard Botanical Museum, 36
hat, Tibetan, 133*f*, 142
health, history of, database on, 84
Heinz Galleries, 29
Heritage Preservation, 6, 153
Hippocrates, 62
historical archives, 101–15
Historical Society of Pennsylvania,
    39–55; contact information for,
    156; founding of, 41–42; and
    public, 46–47
Hodge, Hugh Lenox, 63
Hope Diamond, 81
Houston Museum of Fine Arts,
    45
Hrdlička, Aleš, 71–72, 78–79
human remains, policy on, 83

Imperial Academy Leopoldina, 31
Independence Hall, 7
industrial labor unions, Gowen and,
    39–55
Institute of Museum and Library
    Services, 6, 153
institutions. *See* collecting
    institutions
Internet, and access to treasures,
    152. *See also* digital inventory
inventory, 97. *See also* digital
    inventory
iron lung, 61, 66

jacket, 142
Jackson, Chevalier, 65
Jackson, Stonewall, 125
Jefferson, Thomas, 12, 21, 51
Joseph, Leo, 19–22

Ker-Feal, 85–100, 85*f*
Khan, Kublai, 137

labels, 37, 146–47
labor unions, Gowen and, 39–55
Latrobe, Benjamin, 106
Laughton, Charles, 88
Lee, Robert E., 124, 131
Lenni Lenape, 42, 52
Lewis, Meriwether, 12, 21
Lhasa, 140–41
limeys, term, 76
Lincoln, Abraham, 108, 120
Lincoln, Mary Todd, 121
Lincoln University, 93–95
Lind, James, 76
Lindquist, Fred, 50
Lippincott, Louise, 29–30, 32–38
Little, Cynthia, 46–49, 52–55
living communities, museums and, 135, 147–50
Livingston, David, 21

management issues, 6–7, 28, 151
managers, 49
Manouvrier, Leon, 79
Mao Tse-tung, 140
masks, Tibetan, 144–46
material culture, 1–8
McArthur, John, Jr., 114
McGuire, Hunter Holmes, 125
Meade, George Gordon, 120–21
medical artifacts, 57–68, 57*f*
Medical College of Pennsylvania, 64
Meigs, Montgomery Cunningham, 125
Meigs, S. F., 125–26
Meirs, C. H., 125
Mengele, Josef, 83
Merychyus minimus, 29
Milex Silicone pessary, 63
Military Order of the Loyal Legion of the United States, 120, 126–27

miners, Bowen and, 43–44
Mitchell, S. Weir, 64
Molly Maguires, 43–44
Mona Kachung, 141
Moss, Roger, 103–5, 107, 109, 112–14
Moyamensing, 106
Mummers, 7
museums. *See* collecting institutions
museums studies, 49
Mütter, Thomas Dent, 64
Mütter Museum, 57–68, 57*f*; contact information for, 152, 156

names, Tibetan, 136–37
Nason, James, 135–36, 143–46, 148–50
National Endowment for the Arts, 97
National Endowment for the Humanities, 46
National Museum of Natural History, 69–84; contact information for, 157
National Museum of the American Indian Act, 83
National Register of Historic Places, 99
Native Americans, 42, 52, 76, 144, 146–47
Native Americans Graves Protection and Repatriation Act, 83, 148–49
natural history: Academy of Natural Sciences, 9–22; Carnegie Museum of, 25, 35; National Museum of, 69–84
New-York Historical Society, 53
Nightingale, Florence, 61
not-for-profit organizations, management of, 6

Oates, Stephen B., 122
objects, 1–8; labels for, 37; preservation of, 153; significance of, 2, 53, 55, 152

Old Baldy, 120–21
Old St. Paul's Church, 115
Ord, George, 15, 17
Origins, 81–82
Ortner, Donald, 72–74, 76–77, 79–80, 82
Ott, Stanley, 95

Pacific Voices, 146–47
paleoepidemiology, 84
paleopathology, 72–77, 79–80
Patent Office, 109
Patrick, Ruth, 12
Peale, Charles Willson, 7, 42
Peale, Titian Ramsay, 21
Peary, Robert E., 12
pemmican, 76
Penn, William, 42
Pennsylvania Hospital, 64
Pennsylvania Railroad, 114
Peruvian child, skull of, 69–84, 69*f*
pessaries, 57–68, 57*f*; history of, 62–63; types of, 61
Pew Charitable Trusts, 95
Philadelphia: and Civil War, 120, 126, 128–31; collecting institutions of, 7, 113–14
Philadelphia and Reading Railroad, 42–43
Philadelphia Architects and Buildings Project, 115
Philadelphia City Hall, 114
philanthropy, 113–14; Carnegie on, 26–27; Girard and, 106
philosophy: of community involvement, 149–50; on exhibits, 37; on museums, 49
Phunstok Palace, 138–40
physical anthropology, 77–79
Physick, Philip Syng, 63–64
pike, of John Brown, 117–31, 117*f*

Pinkerton, Allan, 43–44
preservation, 153
presidents, 41, 47–48; turnover of, 22
professional development director, 94–95
provenance, research on, 97
public: Civil War Museum and, 127–28, 131; versus collections, 152; community involvement and, 146–50; and de-accessioning, 52; historical archives and, 104–5; Historical Society of Pennsylvania and, 46–47; market research on, 5; and Mütter Museum, 64–65, 67; and preservation, 153; versus research, 19–22
Putschar, Walter, 77

racism, scientific, 78–79
radiology, 82
Ray, Jeffrey, 1–3, 6, 153
registrars, 97
research: versus exhibitions, 19–22, 46; libraries, 48; medical artifacts and, 66; on provenance, 97
restoration, 32, 112
Reynolds, John F., 120
Rice, Nate, 11
Rockefeller Foundation, 143
Rockwell, Norman, 5
Rohan, Camille de, 30
Rosenblatt, Paul, 37
Ross, Betsy, 7
Royal Botanical Garden, Dresden, 30
Rush, Benjamin, 64

St. Elizabeth's Hospital, 109
Sakya, Jamyang, summer garments of, 133–50, 133*f*

Sakya, Jigdal Dagchen, 136–40, 142–44, 147–48
Sakya-Khon lineage, 137
Sakya Monastery, 147–48
Say, Thomas, 12
Sbag-ma, 144
scarf, 142
Schwartz, Allyson Y., 111
Sciurus niger, 16
scurvy, 71–77
sea animals, by Blaschkas, 23–38, 23*f*
security issues, 53, 127
shared trust holdings, 150
Siamese twins, 65
Simon Wiesenthal Foundation, 83
Siphonophora, 23*f*, 32
skeletal remains: of dinosaurs, 21–22; at Mütter Museum, 66; at National Museum of Natural History, 69–84; policy on, 83
skull, of prehistoric Peruvian child, 69–84, 69*f*
Smithson, James, 81
Smithsonian Institution, National Museum of Natural History, 69–84, 157
soap woman, 65
Sommers, G. N. J., 65
Sonam Tshe Dzom. *See* Sakya, Jamyang
South Kensington Museum, 31
staff, 127; curatorial, 64; and exhibits, 33; and reorganization, 48, 52
stakeholders, 5. *See also* public
Stein, Julie, 149
Stenomylus, 29
stewardship, 53–54, 149
Still, William, 130
Stitt, Susan, 41, 47–55
storage areas, open, 152

Strickland, William, 105–6
Suquamish people, 146

textiles, at Ker-Feal, 98
thangkas, 146
theft, 54
Thomas-Cutter stem pessary, 61
Tibet: character of, 136; names in, 136–37; princess of, summer garments of, 133–50, 133*f*
tourism, in Philadelphia, 7–8
toy train, 2, 153
Tredegar National Civil War Center, 128–29

Underground Railroad, 126. *See also* Civil War and Underground Railroad Museum of Philadelphia
United States capitol, dome of, plan for, 101–15, 101*f*
United States Treasury, 109
United Steel Corporation, 26
University of Washington, 135, 143

Van Gogh Museum, 29, 32–34
visitors: role of, 153. *See also* public
volunteers, 127

Walter, Thomas Ustick: background of, 103, 105–7; buildings of, 114–15; plan for dome of the United States capitol, 101–15, 101*f*
Ward's Natural Science Establishment, 34
Warhol (Andy) Museum, 38
War Library and Museum of the Military Order of the Loyal Legion of the United States. *See* Civil War and Underground Railroad Museum of Philadelphia

Washington, George, 42, 110–11

White, Josiah, 44

William Penn Foundation, 130

Wilson, Alexander, 15

Winterthur, 92

Worden, Gretchen, 59–62, 66–68

Workingmen's Benevolent Association, 43–44

Wylie, Turrell V., 143

yak butter, 139–40

Young Naturalists society, 143

ABOUT THE AUTHOR

A former museum director, **Nancy Moses** has spent much of her career bringing history to light—and to life. Her articles and opinion pieces on civic heritage have appeared in the *Wall Street Journal*, *Philadelphia Inquirer*, *Boston Globe*, and other publications.

Nancy served as a delegate to the White House Conference on Travel and Tourism and to President Clinton's Summit on Volunteerism. She holds a master's degree in American civilization from The George Washington University and lives in Philadelphia's historic Society Hill along with her husband, Myron, and poodle, Frederick.